EARLY IRISH LITERATURE

EARLY IRISH LITERATURE

ELEANOR KNOTT
GERARD MURPHY

Introduction by
JAMES CARNEY

LONDON
ROUTLEDGE & KEGAN PAUL

Published 1966
by Routledge & Kegan Paul Limited
Broadway House, 68–74 Carter Lane
London, E.C.4

Printed in Great Britain by
Western Printing Services Limited
Bristol

© *Government of Ireland*

2nd impression 1967

Contents

SAGA AND MYTH IN ANCIENT IRELAND

THE OSSIANIC LORE AND ROMANTIC TALES OF MEDIEVAL IRELAND

Abbreviations

Duanaire Finn, III = Irish Texts Society, vol. xliii, by
      Gerard Murphy.

RC   = *Revue celtique.*

R.I.A.   = The Royal Irish Academy
      (Dublin).

TBC   = J. Strachan and J. G. O'Keeffe,
      *The Táin Bó Cúailnge from
      the Yellow Book of Lecan with
      Variant Readings from the
      Lebor na hUidre* (1912).

Thurneysen, *Heldensage* = Rudolf Thurneysen, *Die irische
      Helden- und Königsage* (1921).

ZCP   = *Zeitschrift für celtische Philologie.*

Introduction[1]

IN the present volume are brought together three important works on early Irish literature: *Irish Classical Poetry*, by Dr. Eleanor Knott; *Saga and Myth in Ancient Ireland* and *The Ossianic Lore and Romantic Tales of Medieval Ireland*, by the late Professor Gerard Murphy.[2] Between them, these three works by two most distinguished Celticists, comprise an excellent introduction to over a thousand years of traditional Gaelic literature, reckoning from its remote beginnings in the sixth or seventh century down to the eighteenth, by which time the production of creative literature in traditional forms had come almost to a standstill.

Of the two authors Dr. Knott had perhaps the easier task. In 1922 and 1926, in two volumes of the publications of the Irish Texts Society, she produced an edition of the bardic poems of Tadhg Dall Ó hUiginn. This was a work of consummate scholarship, and I think it can be fairly said that all scholars who have dealt with this subject since that date have been deeply in Dr. Knott's debt. Here, for the first time, we were presented with the entire surviving corpus of the work of a traditional poet, together with a close examination of his vocabulary, his technique, his background and place in society. Dr. Knott's work on this poet is important not merely as a detailed presentation of the sixteenth century Tadhg Dall: it has an even greater

---

[1] The translations from Irish in the Introduction are by the present writer.

[2] In bringing together these three works in a single volume it has been necessary to make a few minor changes in expression. These changes, resulting from a mere mechanical necessity, have been made silently by me.

importance in the fact that, owing to the conservatism of the Irish poetic order, in learning about Tadhg Dall we learn inferentially about his contemporaries and about his predecessors for many hundred years; indeed, in some ways in studying Tadhg Dall or any classical poet we are brought into contact with pre-history, for the poets have, as Dr. Knott has pointed out, an uninterrupted descent from the pre-Christian druidic order.

Much close work remains to be done on Irish literature, and meanwhile generalizations are very dangerous. It must, however, be stressed that there is no such thing as a literature which is Irish, pure and uncontaminated. The literature that we know came into being mainly as a result of the impact upon primitive Irish society of Christianity and of Graeco-Latin civilization. The cross-fertilization took place at a period that ante-dates our earliest literary monuments, and there is no piece of literature that can be taken without question as an accurate reflection of Ireland's pagan past.

If we were to point to one fact that changed the whole development of literature in Ireland we would, I think, point to the monastic reform initiated by the Cistercians in the twelfth century. Up to this point the monasteries had been a main-stay of literary production in the vernacular. After this period it is almost as if the monasteries cleaned their cupboards of secular or semi-secular manuscripts, bringing the monks back with a jolt to things more closely connected with salvation than the deeds of Cú Chulainn. From this period on the guardianship of the manuscript remains of early Irish literature, as well as the continuation of productivity in this field, falls increasingly on the great Irish literary families who, quite suddenly, came into prominence about the thirteenth century. In all this there was gain as well as loss. In the early monastic period, as well as being Irish or 'Celtic', the literature produced in Ireland could also be called European. After laicization the external element, though never lost, becomes muter. Irish literature now draws more freely on one of its original springs, that curious society that was barbaric, aristocratic, cattle-stealing, but which nevertheless could show at times a delicate and penetrating sensitivity even in a general milieu of raucousness and bombast. From all this comes the paradox that later Irish literature tends to be more 'primitive' than that of the earlier period. A saga such as the fourteenth-century Battle of Ventry is less sophisticated than *Táin Bó Cúailnge*, *Togail Bruidne Da Derga*, or *Scéla Cano meic Gartnáin*. There is a general crudity of style, a slapstick humour and an insensitivity to the finer points of characterization: the elements that tended to control or soften such features are no longer so potent.

At this point we may ask: why is there, generally speaking, a greater appreciation of the Irish poetry produced before the Norman invasion than of that produced in the four centuries or so that succeeded it? The answer, it seems to me, is something like this. In the later period there are some well-constructed poems, showing sensitivity and subtlety. But they are invariably marred in some degree by standardization of form, of expression and by a highly uneconomic use of words. In the better products of the early period words are used economically, and a situation is realised with intensity and some psychological insight. There is available an amazingly wide variety of metrical forms which, at this period, are still sufficiently loose to put the minimum of constraint on the poet; furthermore this period would appear to be one of metrical experiment, and a poet can create a form suitable to the mood of his poem. Above all there is freshness and an avoidance of the cliché. As an example we may mention the song of Liadan when she remembers her lover Cuirithir,[1] probably the

---

[1] This poem is embedded in a prose saga. One must exercise great care in using the prose in order to interpret such a poem. It would, I think, be easy to show that in such sagas as *Liadan and Cuirithir* and *Scéla Cano meic Gartnáin*

3

finest love poem in Irish literature. The poem appears to
belong to the ninth century:

Cen áinius
in gním hí do-rigénus,
an ro-charus ro-cráidius . . .

No pleasure
that deed I did, tormenting him,
tormenting what I treasure.

Joyfully,
but that God had come between us then
had I granted what he begged of me.

Not unwise
is the way that he is taking now,
enduring pain and gaining Paradise.

Great folly
where once I showed such gentleness
to set Cuirithir against me!

Liadan I;
they say that I loved Cuirithir,
nor would I, if I could, deny.

The while I bless
that I was in his company
and was treating him with tenderness.

A woodland breeze
was my melody with Cuirithir,
Sounding harmony of reddening seas.

It seemed thus:
the last thing I would ever do
was a deed to come between us.

---

the poetry and prose are not a single unit. The poetry survived alone, probably
in manuscript; the writer of the saga used the older verse and sometimes
misunderstood or misplaced it. In such cases the verse often reveals a much
more sophisticated mind than the prose.

Cry clearly:
if any lovers this heart cherishes,
he its darling, loved most dearly.

A cry of pain
and the heart within was rent in two,
without him never beats again.

Meyer has said: 'To seek out and watch nature, in its tiniest phenomena as in its grandest, was given to no people so early and so fully as to the Celt. Many hundreds of Gaelic and Welsh poems testify to this fact. It is a characteristic of these poems that in none of them do we get an elaborate or sustained description of any scene or scenery, but rather a succession of pictures and images which the poet, like an impressionist, calls up before us by light and skilful touches. Like the Japanese, the Celts were always quick to take an artistic hint; they avoid the obvious and the commonplace; the half-said thing to them is the dearest.'[1]

This impressionism, which Meyer noted is characteristic of the early period, but not of the later. An excellent example is the well-known poem on Winter:

Scél lemm dúib:
dordaid dam,
snigid gaim,
ro fáith sam . . .

News I bring:
bells the stag,
winter snow,
summer past;

wind high and cold,
low the sun,
short its course,
seas are strong;

---

[1] Selections from *Ancient Irish Poetry*, p. xii.

russet bracken,
shape awry,
wild goose raises
wonted cry;
cold lays hold
on wings of bird,
icy time:
this I heard.

In this poem the poet, the bearer of the 'news', is like an impressionist painter. But there is no human element within his picture, nobody to experience it or to contemplate the scene. By contrast, in the following ninth-century poem, it is the human experience that is important:

Dom-farcai fidbaidae fál,
fom-chain loíd luin, lúad nád chél;
húas mo lebrán, ind línech,
fom-chain trírech inna n-én.

Fomm-chain coí menn—medair mass—
hi mbrot glass di dindgnaib doss.
Débrath, nom-choimmdiu-coíma,
caín-scríbaimm fo roída ross.

A wall of forest looms above,
and sweetly the blackbird sings;
all the birds make melody
over me and my books and things.

There sings to me the cuckoo
from bush-citadel in grey hood.
God's doom! May the Lord protect me,
writing well, under the great wood.

I think that it is too often assumed that the early Irish monk always felt himself at one with nature. Despite certain poems that show this, there was another attitude which is present in the poem I have just quoted: that nature is the antithesis of settled monastic life and is at variance with it: hence the poet finds the forest menacing and the cuckoo is a

6

warrior threatening him from bush-citadels; he must seek God's protection against all this distracting and enervating beauty. The monk living in an ecclesiastical 'city' is an urban character who has abandoned a life that, in retrospect, is wild, beautiful and free. This attitude is clearly shown in the monk's envy of the blackbird:

> Och, a luin, is buide duit,
> cáit sa muine i fuil do net,
> a díthrebaig nád clinn cloc,
> is binn boc síthemail th'fet.

> Alas, blackbird, it is well for you,
> wherever in the thicket be your nest,
> hermit that sounds no bell,
> sweet, soft and fairylike is your note.

The monastery bell was symbolic of settled monastic society, and the abandonment of the world, the flesh and the devil:

> Clocán binn
> benar i n-aidchi gaíthe,
> ba ferr lemm dul ina dáil
> indás i ndáil mná baíthe.

> Melodious bell
> that is struck on a night of wind,
> I had rather make tryst with it
> than with wanton womankind.

Nowhere is the conflict of monastic Ireland on one side, and rural Ireland on the other so well shown as in the twelfth-century saga of Buile Śuibne. Here, indeed, matters have gone so far that the reader is invited to take a pro-nature, anti-monastic stand:

> Ba binne lium ro bhaoí tan
> ná guth cluigín im fharradh
> ceileabhradh an luin don bheinn
> is dordán doimh ar doininn.

. . . .

Ba binne lium ro bhaoí tan
donálach na gcon alla
iná guth cléirigh as-toigh
ag méiligh is ag meigeallaigh.

There was a time I thought more sweet
than the voice of a little bell beside me
the singing of the blackbird from the hill,
the belling of a stag in the storm.

There was a time I thought more sweet
the howling of the wolves
than the voice of a cleric within
a-baaing and a-bleating.

In following this thought we can see literature stealing out of the monasteries and in the process becoming mildly anti-clerical.

A point that must be made clear about early Irish poetry is that a large part of it was produced by a society of considerable sophistication. We must, indeed, emphasize this, for the very reason that many modern scholars have failed to perceive it. The study of this literature is too often bedevilled by an eighteenth/nineteenth-century romanticism that idealizes the 'primitive' and likes to look upon the early Irish writer as almost a passive traditor of ancient thoughts and ideas of which he himself had no fully conscious understanding. Hence, an early Irish poem need not always be expected to make full sense, and the most outrageous translations can be thought possible. We must, I think, be more humble in our approach to these early poets. They were, at times, as sophisticated as the scholars who in modern times have undertaken the edition and translation of their works. Indeed, I would state the following as a useful working principle: when we approach an early Irish poem, finally achieving a translation, if the result in some way gives less than full sense, the fault is more likely to lie in our own method and understanding than in the naïveté of the ancient poet. To achieve the optimum understanding of this poetry we must first learn to approach it with respect and humility.

Elsewhere I have written in an essay:[1] '. . . in the Old Irish period a group of academic Christian gentlemen were composing subjective verse of a high order. That these men were academic is shown as much by the content of their verses as by the fact that their poems are preserved on the margins of great ecclesiastical codices. A feature of their verse is their academic delight in learned riddle, paradox, contrast, and elaborate metaphor.'

A feature mentioned in the same essay, but not stressed, was the sophisticated humour of these poets. This is shown very delicately in the poem quoted above on the scholar reading out-of-doors. It is also shown in the well-known poem on Pangur Bán, the monk's pet cat. But this is not primarily a poem on a cat. It is the monk's humorous evaluation of himself, a caution against taking his academic pursuits too seriously. In trying to understand his texts by ploughing through dictionaries and word-lists he is no better than a cat chasing mice. Indeed, for the scholar the comparison is as forceful and as salutary in our society today as when the poem was first written almost twelve centuries ago.

Despite extremes of asceticism humour could enter into the religion of the early Irish. In a poem written about A.D. 1000 a poet puts himself in the dock on a charge of allowing his mind to wander in strange and unseemly places during the singing of the psalms. Indeed, it is possible that the poem formed in his mind during one of these long periods of community prayer, and would thus be part of the substance of his sin:

> *Is mebul dom imrádud*
> *a méit élas uaimm;*
> *ad-águr a imgábud*
> *i lló brátha buain . . .*

[1] *Early Irish Society*, ed. Myles Dillon, p. 74.

A shame on my thinking,
 how it wanders away;
it will cause me embarrassment
 on Last Judgement day.

At psalm-time it rushes forth
 on a pathway that's odd,
running, raving, misbehaving
 in the presence of God.

To merry women's company,
 the unvirtuous kind,
through wood and through cities
 faster than the wind.

When road is smooth it travels
 merrily and gay,
but passes just as easily
 the impenetrable way.

It needs no ship to journey
 and the seas go by,
jumps with but a single leap
 from solid earth to sky.

No course of wisdom does it run
 whether near or far
and after all foolishness
 it's back where we are.

Put a fetter on its leg,
 chain it to prayer?
Yes! But in a minute's time
 it's no longer there.

Little use in beating it,
 plying whip or rod:
like an eel's tail it slips away
 from my grasp and from God.

No chain and no dark dungeon
 will hinder its course;
it laughs at seas and fortresses,
 is mocking of force.

O dear Christ, lord of chastity,
    chain thinking in place
with power of Spirit septiform
    and all His grace.

Make, O great elemental God,
    the heart be still,
that you be my only love
    and I your will.

May I come to Christ at last
    and then to see
that He is no unsteady thing,
    not wandering like me.

Much detailed work remains to be done on Irish poetry, particularly, perhaps, in examining the thoughts and ideas of the traditional 'bardic' poets. But in the study of Irish poetry there are no basic controversies, no virtually irreconcilable views. From the very beginnings of Irish literature we can confidently associate certain poems with names: Dallán Forgaill wrote the *Amra Coluim Chille* about 597; Blathmac mac Con Brettan wrote poems to the Blessed Virgin about 750; Oengus Céle Dé wrote his *Félire* about 800; Airbertach Mac Coise is the probable author of *Saltair na Rann*, written towards the close of the tenth century; Mael Ísa Ó Brolcháin wrote lyrics in the second half of the eleventh; meanwhile traditional history was being written by a number of poets whose names and dates are known; in later times, from the thirteenth to the seventeenth century, we can associate a considerable number of poems with specific authors such as Muireadhach Albanach Ó Dálaigh, Giolla Brighde Mac Con Midhe, Tadhg Dall Ó hUiginn, and Eochaidh Ó hEodhusa. From these and others we can form a picture of the varying types of people from whom derive the manuscript remains of Irish poetry.

Prose offers a great contrast. I think it is true to say that there is no early saga of which it can be said that it was given its extant form by this personality or that.[1] This, in fact, is what makes Professor Murphy's task so much more difficult and controversial than Dr. Knott's. His problem, in any given case, begins with the work itself which, as it were, suddenly appears from nowhere. What is its origin? When was it 'written down'? What was its purpose? Are we dealing with the vestiges of religious myth, with legend, with history of a kind, or with a mixture of all three? The saga tradition of Ireland and the Irish oral tale that has survived down to our own day, together with the thoughts and ideas that lie behind them, stand in need of so much close investigation that most conclusions are premature and virtually all generalizations perilous.

Irish saga literature may be divided roughly into the following groups:

1. Mythological tales in which the characters are quite clearly divinities of the Irish pagan period such as In Dagda, 'The Good God', otherwise known as Eochaid Ollathair, Eochaid, 'the Great Father', his son Oengus or Maccind Óc, Midir, the latter's rival in love.

2. Tales of the Ulster heroes at the court of Conchobar at a period reckoned by early Irish historians, on a very dubious and obscure basis, as being contemporary with the beginning of the Christian era.

3. Tales of Finn mac Cumaill and the *fiana* (warrior bands). The period of these tales was thought to be coincident with the reign of Cormac, son of Art, placed by early historians in the third century of the Christian era. There is a general cultural contrast between the Ulster tales and the Finn tales. In the former the heroes live in a state of barbaric magnificence, using the chariot, and their only avocation is war. In the Finn tales the heroes are normally in the forest, they are primarily hunters, and go on foot.

---

[1] I hope, however, in the future to give reasons that might point to Rumann, son of Colmán, who died in 746, as the personality who first gave saga form to Táin Bó Cúailnge .

4. 'King tales', that is, tales of dynastic origins and of the deeds of kings and nobles, mostly set well within the historic period.

5. Tales of expeditions (*Echtrai*) to the Otherworld such as *Echtrae Condlai*; tales of voyages such as *Immram Brain maic Febail*. Both these tales are set in the pre-Christian period, but most of this type, such as the Voyage of Mael Dúin, are set against a Christian background. One of the most important examples of this type is the Latin *Navigatio Brendani*, which was to have considerable effect on medieval literature and thought.

These categories cover the greater part of Irish saga in the early period, although there are a number of tales that would not fit easily into any of them. The categories are not absolute: In *Táin Bó Fraích* and *Aislinge Óengusso*, for instance, the 'gods' of category (1) mix freely with the men of category (2). Similarly in incident: The story of *Longas mac nUislenn* is the presentation of a theme most widely known in *Tristan and Isolde* in terms of characters of the Ulster cycle. The story of Diarmait and Gráinne is a presentation of the same theme in terms of characters of the Finn cycle. *Scéla Cano meic Gartnáin* and the love story of Liadan and Cuirithir present the same theme in terms of historical characters of the seventh century.

It is impossible here to deal at any great length with the problem of the nature of this literature, so I shall confine myself to some few comments on the theory of euhemerization, which, in our day, tends to dominate thinking on the subject.

In pagan Ireland, as in all primitive societies, we may say with certainty that there existed tales of gods, religious myths that in some way gave sanction to and controlled the *mores* of society. With the advent of Christianity, and the gradual overthrow of pagan belief, many of these ancient gods, according to current theories, were euhemerized: that is, they were presented as historical characters, and there would, of course, have been considerable modification in the stories related of them. It is very likely, indeed, that our early and medieval literature is partly a result of this process of euhemerization, but it is very difficult to assess how widespread the process has been. Hence it would be hazardous, at the present stage of Irish studies, to deny emphatically that Cú Chulainn, Medb, Conchobar and others were originally gods. But it would be equally hazardous to assert it strongly, as does O'Rahilly in his *Early Irish History and Mythology*. Without taking too decided a view of the matter I must confess that in my own mind the balance tips somewhat against the assumption of euhemerization on a very great scale: it is an idea that enjoys a vogue and which, whatever amount of truth may underlie it, appears to be over-used.

In this whole matter perhaps the best case has been made for regarding Medb as a dethroned goddess. This theory, first put forward by Tomás Ó Máille,[1] has been widely accepted, and was developed further by O'Rahilly.[2]

The case rests fundamentally on the well-known idea of kingship-marriage, that is, that in primitive Irish thinking an Irish dynast, on attaining kingship, was wedded to the sovereignty, which was conceived of as a goddess. Medb, we are to believe, was the goddess of Tara whom every successive Tara King married symbolically.

There is no direct evidence to link Medb of Cruachain with whatever goddess originally symbolized the sovereignty of Tara. The evidence mainly rests (a) on an etymologizing of her name, and (b) on identifying her with another Medb, Medb Leithderg, who, it is assumed, was such a goddess.

Ó Máille's original contribution was brilliant, and I have no intention of saying that he was wrong, but merely that I am left in doubt.

First we will glance at the significance of the name. It contains the root *med-*, found in Irish *mid*, English 'mead',

[1] ZCP, XVII, pp. 129–46. [2] *Ériu*, XIV, pp. 15–21.

etc. According to Thurneysen the name meant 'the intoxicated one' (could it not also merely mean 'the mead-possessing one'?). Ó Máille and O'Rahilly, however, prefer to take the name in an active sense, 'the intoxicating one', an idea which will better support an association with the ceremony of kingship-marriage.

We then come to an assumption which we may regard as quite likely: 'that in pagan times the acceptance by the bridegroom of a draught of liquor handed to him by the bride signified mutual consent to the marriage.'[1] From here we go on to the conclusion that Medb, 'she who intoxicates', has come by this descriptive name because it was she who, at the kingship-marriage, was supposed to hand a cup of mead to her would-be spouse, thereby making him king.

It should, I think, have been pointed out that in the earliest occurrences of the name Medb we have to do, not with a woman, but with a man. In an ogam inscription found in Rathcroghan, precisely the area with which Medb of Cruachain is associated as queen, we find Vraicci maqi Medvvi,[2] 'of Vraiccos, son of Medvos'.[3] Similarly we find a fifth-century priest (who was presumably born a pagan) called by Tírechán presbyter Medb.[4]

From this we can draw certain conclusions. In pagan Ireland the name that we know in Old Irish as Medb was quite common. It was found in a masculine form Medvos

[1] Ériu, XIV, p. 15.

[2] Macalister, Corpus Inscriptionum Insularum Celticarum, I, p. 16.

[3] That is, giving the names their Old Irish forms, 'of Froích, son of Medb'. In Irish tradition one Froích is a son of Fidach of the Gamanraid. He would appear to have been an important dynast, for it was upon Carnfree ('The burial mound of Froích') that kings of Cruachain were inaugurated. In the traditions assembled by Ó Máille, this Fidach of the Gamanraid is a suitor (unsuccessful) for the hand of Medb. One cannot help wondering if the ogam inscription does not fit somewhere into this complex of tradition. Could the traditional Medb have originally been a man?

[4] Stokes, Tripartite Life of St. Patrick, p. 337. In the same source Sadb is also found as a man's name.

and in a feminine *Medva*. In the traditions that have survived concerning the association of liquor with the ceremony
of kingship-marriage the liquor commonly found is ale,
whether described as *coirm* or *laith* (*flaith*). There is not, so
far as I am aware, any specific reference to mead in this
connection. The commonness of the name *Medb* and the
existence of a masculine form certainly do not suggest that
in early Ireland *Medb* would immediately conjure up the
idea of the goddess-queen of Tara.

In the tradition of Medb Leithderg we read that she
married nine kings of Tara, in fact, that she would not
allow anyone who did not marry her to become king.
While somewhere at the back of such traditions we may well
have the very common idea of kingship-marriage, this is by
no means certain. We must allow for the Irish tendency to
exaggerate. Before interpreting such traditions it would, I
think, be salutary to look at the historical queen Gormlaith
(†946), and to ask ourselves what the mythologizers would
have made of her if she had lived before the strictly historic
period.

First there is the matter of her name. *Gormlaith* means
either 'Red Ale' or else 'Dark Sovereignty'.[1] Whichever
meaning one chooses it is a perfect name for a kingship-
goddess in her function as the pourer of the liquor of
sovereignty. Gormlaith was a daughter of Flann Sinna,
king of Tara and of Ireland. She married successively
three kings: Cerball of Leinster, Cormac of Cashel, and
finally Niall Glúndub, king of Ireland. Had the tradition
of this woman come to us by hundreds of years of oral
tradition, confused with other queens of the same name,
we might easily hear that she had a dozen husbands, all
kings, and that she allowed no one to be king who did not
marry her.

I must again emphasize that in the foregoing comments

---

[1] It is a compound of *gorm* 'blue', etc., and *flaith* 'sovereignty' or *laith*
'liquor'. Possibly the double meaning was intended.

I am not rejecting the theory that certain characters presented in Irish tradition as historical are, in fact, euhemerized deities. On the contrary I must admit to being impressed, for instance, by Murphy's work on the character of Finn mac Cumaill in his voluminous notes and comments in *Duanaire Finn*. But a stage has come in Irish studies when characters in tradition are made into gods, goddesses, or 'ancestor-deities' on the slenderest evidence. I would like my comments here to be regarded as a plea for the development in the future of a better and more convincing methodology. Every saga requires careful analytic study, and every other saga, anecdote or tradition used to elucidate it must itself be subjected to scrutiny and analysis. This is a daunting programme, but only by working along these lines can we minimize the subjectivity which is a hazard confronting any investigator of the origins of Irish literature and tradition.[1]

[1] I am far from suggesting that my analysis of Táin Bó Fraích (*Studies in Irish Literature and History*, pp. 1–76) achieves the ideal in methodology. I may, however, be permitted to mention it as a striving towards the method that I recommend.

I

IRISH CLASSICAL POETRY
Commonly called Bardic Poetry

I. Early Poetry

THE beginnings of classical or 'bardic' Irish poetry lie far back in our history. Both in form and content we see the mingling of varied influences, Christian and pagan. In early documents we meet the terms *bard* and *bairdne*, *fili* and *filidecht*; during the Middle Irish period, that is after the late tenth century, *bard* and *bairdne* became rare, but *fili* and *filidecht*, 'poet' and 'poetry', persist in common use down to modern times.

The distinction between *bard* and *fili* in the earlier period is still an obscure subject and has not been fully investigated. Here we can merely say that according to the early metrical tracts the *bard* was simply a poet and versifier;[1] the *fili* a poet, but also a scholar and guardian of traditional knowledge; he is especially a prophet and a seer and can wield supernatural powers. In short, he somewhat resembles in his functions the druid of pre-Christian Gaul. In the literature we find at times that *fili* and *druí* (druid) are interchangeable terms.

The druids of Gaul studied their art in Britain, and it is noteworthy that it was to Britain also, according to our legends, that the candidate *fili* resorted to qualify in the art of divination. Thus we read of Néde, son of Adna, *ollam Éirenn i n-écsi & fhilidecht* 'the ollave of Ireland in divination and poetry': *Luid in mac sin do fhoglaim écsi i nAlbain* 'That

---

[1] Compare the respective status of *joglar* and *troubadour*: 'The *joglar* was one who made a business of poetry and music, both popular and aristocratic; the *troubadour* was one who composed aristocratic poetry . . .', Chaytor's *The Troubadours of Dante* (Oxford 1902), p. xiii. See also below, p. 6off.

boy went to study divination in Albu' (i.e., Albion, Britain; the modern restricted application of the name is of later origin). Similarly, Fedelm *banfhili* 'F. the woman-*fili*,' who encounters Medb on the eve of the Táin, replies to the question whence has she come? *A hAlbain iar foglaim filidechta* 'From Albu after studying *filidecht*' (which here, by the context, also means 'divination'). Both *éicse* and *filidecht* are frequently found with the meaning 'poetry' in early documents, but the connotation 'occult gifts and practices' is also well attested. The early conflict between the church and the *fili* was not in the rivalry between sacred and secular literature, but between Christianity and druidism. The Colloquy between Néde (mentioned above) and Ferchertne, the contestants for the Chair of Poetry, is not in syllabic verse, but in a kind of rhythmic prose abounding in 'kennings' and words obsolete apparently in the eleventh century or earlier. The disputants themselves are said to have been contemporary with Conchobar mac Nessa, whom the annals make contemporary with Tiberius, but we are here in the obscure region of pre-Patrician history and cannot give precise dates.

The differences between church and *fili* were smoothed out eventually. Individuals passed from one following to the other: the patron saint of Cloyne, Colmán son of Lénéne, had been a *fili* before he took holy orders. Some verses ascribed to him are quoted in glossaries and he was the teacher of Dálach, from whom the famous (and in one of its scions, infamous) poet family of Uí Dálaigh are descended. But churchman and *fili*, though often identical in a composer of verse, remained separate categories. The official *fili* apparently took over some of the functions of the early bard in addition to his own duties of preserving and teaching secular tradition, metrics, grammar, etc. That the tradition of the *fili* as prophet, judge and historian, as well as poet, persisted until the latest period of the native culture, is witnessed to by an external observer, the apothecary

Thomas Smyth, resident in Dublin in 1651. In his 'Information for Ireland', he states: 'Their is in Ireland four shepts in Maner all Rimers. The firste of them is calleid the Brehounde, which in English is calleid the Judge . . . The second sourte is the Shankee, which is to saye in English the Petigrer [=pedigreer] . . . The thirde sorte is called the aeosdan [= *aos dán*], which is to saye in English the bards or the riming septces . . . The fourth sort of Rymers is called fillis [i.e. *filidh*, pl. of *fili*], which is to saye in English a poete. Theis men have great store of cattell and use all the trades of the others with an adicion of prophecies.' Compare with this last sentence the description of Tadhg Ó Huiginn, *Annals of Connacht* 1315: *sai chotchend cech cerdi da mbenand re filidecht* 'general master of all arts connected with *filidecht*'.

Smyth's description, though unsympathetic in tone, is on the whole accurate. We shall have occasion to quote further from it later on. In the meantime, we must turn to the subject of form.[1]

METRICAL FORM

Although Ireland, happily or unhappily, was never invaded by the Roman legions, or came under the sway of the Roman emperor, the literary legacy of Rome was not withheld from her. Christianity and Latin learning were inseparable. Whether Meyer was right or not in his theory that the 'rethorici' apostrophized by Patrick (Conf. 13) were Gaulish rhetors who had taken refuge in Ireland from the troubles of Europe,[2] there is no doubt about the cultivation

[1] See further G. Murphy's 'Bards and filidh', *Éigse*, ii, 200 f. For Néde and the Colloquy see Stokes's edition, *Revue celtique*, xxvi, 4 f. For Colmán son of Lénéne and his poems see Thurneysen, *Zeits. für celtische Philologie*, xix, 193 f., Bergin *Studies*, 1918, 97 f. For Smyth's tract see *Ulster Journal of Archaeology*, vi (1918), 166.
[2] In 'Learning in Ireland in the fifth century . . . A Lecture delivered before the School of Irish Learning . . . 1912'.

of Latin rhetoric in the early Irish schools. However, it is not in the rhetorics, some types of which had an influence more baneful than salutary on Irish literary style, that we shall find the origin of the stately and melodious quatrains of Irish classical poetry, e.g.:

> D'fhior chogaidh comhailltear síothcháin,
> seanfhocal nach sáraighthear;
> ní fhaghann síoth acht fear faghla
> feadh Banbha na mbánfhoithreadh.

This is the opening stanza of an exhortation addressed to Brian na múrtha Ó Ruairc by the most celebrated of the Irish poets of the late sixteenth century, Tadhg Dall Ó Huiginn. The first line of each couplet has eight syllables, the second seven; the longer lines end in a disyllabic word, the shorter in a trisyllabic.[1] The metre is called *séadna mór* by the later prosodists followed by O'Molloy, but in the early Irish metrical tracts it is called *dian midsheng*. The alternation of disyllable and trisyllable (=accented trochee and dactyl) in the line-endings, together with the rule that the end-word of the third line shall rime with the penultimate stressed word of the fourth, gives the stanza a strong and lively rhythm. It is essentially the metre of Cú Chuimne's *Hymn to the Blessed Virgin*:

> Cantemus in omni dìe   concinentes vàrie
> conclamantes Deo dìgnum   ymnum sanctae Màriae.

This hymn, as the Irish Preface in the Liber Hymnorum tells us, is composed in *rithimm (rhythmus)*: it is the *rhythmus* or vulgar Latin version of the trochaic tetrameter catalectic of which the classical form is used in another hymn included in the Irish Liber Hymnorum, the well-known one attributed to Hilary of Poitiers, beginning:

[1] The following rendering is in a rough imitation of the metre, omitting alliteration and some of the internal rime:

> To the warlike peace is preserved, a proverb infallible;
> none hath peace save men in armour throughout Banva brackenfair (lit. of fair thickets).

Hymnum dicat turba fratrum ymnum cantus personet
Christo regi concinentes laudem demus debitam.[1]

The rhythmic form is also found in other Irish-Latin hymns, notably, of course, that of Secundinus, which is unrimed, however. In Thurneysen's view this popular late-Latin measure is that from which, by successive modifications, variations in syllabic length of line and of end-word etc., all other Irish syllabic metres have developed.[2]

From the late Latin rhythms and church sequences, as used and modified by Irish poets, first in Latin (with Irish accentuation) and then in Irish, sprang the 'strict' or *dán díreach* metres which for more than nine centuries were to delight the ears and feed the imagination of Irish listeners.

But the syllabic system is not the only distinctive characteristic of *dán díreach*; rime is also an integral part of it, and the origin of this is not so easily established. It is, as is well known, frequent in Christian Latin poetry and is used in several of the hiberno-latin hymns in the Irish Liber Hymnorum, in the *Altus Prosator* of Colum Cille, and more elaborately in, for instance, the hymn by Cú Chuimne already mentioned, and in that of St. Oengus in praise of St. Martin. Whether it was from the Latin hymns and sequences that rime first came into use in Irish poetry, or whether it was to some extent in use in pre-Christian times has not yet been ascertained, in fact the beginnings of rime in European poetry are still obscure to scholars. Raby, in his *History of Christian Latin poetry* (1953), discussing the use of the *Altus Prosator* by the Carolingian poet Raban Maur (Hrabanus Maurus), remarks that 'it was among the Irish poets that the possibilities of rime and rhythm were most significantly recognized' (pp. 181–183). Some examples of rhythmically stressed rimed verse, apparently of a very early period, are extant, but there is no clear evidence that end-rime was

[1] For these hiberno-latin poems see *The Irish Liber Hymnorum*, edited by Bernard and Atkinson.

[2] But cf. the article 'Indo-European metrics and archaic Irish verse' by Calvert Watkins, *Celtica*, vi, 194 ff.

used by Irish poets before they had come into contact with Christian latinity. In his paper on the oldest Irish poetry (Kgl. Akad. der Wiss., Berlin 1914) Kuno Meyer maintains that rime was not used in Irish verse of the pre-Christian period. He also suggests that a tradition that rime was a relatively late innovation is reflected in a note on p. 311 of the twelfth-century *Book of Leinster*, according to which it was Russ Ruad, father of Finn fili ('Finn the poet'), that 'invented harmony at the ends of poems'. This Russ is recorded as a prehistoric king of Leinster, and, so far as our knowledge of them goes, he and his son remain mythical figures; but Meyer may be right. A version of this note in Rawl. B 502, Facs. 118^{b}3 has, instead of 'poems' (*duan*), the somewhat obscure word *comarc* (*comarg*) which perhaps means 'line', or 'couplet' here. In any case Rawl. has probably the correct reading. There is no doubt that the earlier style of Irish verse was alliterative, rhythmical and rimeless. We have specimens of it in very ancient documents such as early law texts and the older genealogies. And even after the riming, syllable-counting metres had become the established fashion there continued in use to some extent a blend of old and new; rhythmically stressed verses with regularity of syllabic length, rimed or unrimed. There is an example of the unrimed style in the story of the Death of Muirchertach mac Erca[1] in the fourteenth-century *Yellow Book of Lecan*, and a few in *Caithréim Thoirdhelbhaigh*, a tract on the wars of the O'Briens edited for the Irish Texts Society by S. H. O'Grady and Robin Flower, e.g.:

> Togha Temhrach Toirdhelbhach
> mac Taidhg I Bhriain bognáireach
> airdrí Chaisil chlaidhemhdheirg
> lennán Tailten taobhuaine
> maccán Uisnigh órchuachaigh . . .[2]

---

[1] Edited by Stokes, *Revue celtique*, xxiii. In the edition by Lilian Duncan (Dublin, 1964) the verse passages, mostly abbreviated by Stokes, are given in full.

[2] ITS, xxvi, p. 27.

This unrimed style also differs from the regular syllabic in that it is not stanzaic.

Both the texts cited here also include a good deal of verse in the regular syllabic style.

The nature of the rime in Irish syllabic verse is characteristic. It does not consist in identity of vowels and consonants, neither is it mere vowel-rime. There is identity of vowels; not of consonants. These are arranged in classes within which they rime, thus *c*, *t*, *p* form one class, *b*, *d*, *g* another, *ch*, *ph*(*f*), *th* another and so on. We find this system already fully developed by the end of the eighth century; how much earlier it was introduced we cannot tell.

In strict metres, what regularity of rhythm there is, is established by the syllabic length of the end-words in the lines of the stanza. According to the law of stress-accent in Irish a disyllabic word is a trochee, a trisyllabic a dactyl. Only the word-stress matters, and as all words (save the deuterotonic forms of compound verbs, where the pre-verb was felt more as a preposition than as an integral part of the verb) are strongly stressed on the first syllable, there need be no discussion of iambs, anapaests, etc. In the stressed metres in later use, a rime can be made up of two or more words, a slightly heavier stress being given to the first; to take a few instances at random from Keating's poems:

> Do dhorchaigh an ré d'éis bheith lán di
> is do mhúich maise gach leasa 'sgach áruis

Here *lán di* rimes with *áruis*; in *dán díreach* both would have full stress and the rime would be impossible. Similarly:

> Gur tréigeadh leat gidh beart nár dhual duit
> an dream d'fhuiling go minic a dtuargain.

Compare this couplet in strict *deibhidhe*, also attributed to Keating:

> Sgéimh ghlacshoillse gér dhual di,
> snuadh na hathtuirse uirthi.

where *di* rimes with the second syllable of *uirthi* (*deibhidhe*-rime) and *dual* rimes with *snuadh*.

However, I must not linger further on this aspect of our subject. I have given some space to it merely to draw attention to the characteristics which form the distinction between the syllable-counting metres called in Irish *dán díreach* and the metres of a rhythmic character but with a superficial resemblance to the former. The essentials of every *dán díreach* metre are: a line or couplet containing a certain number of syllables; regularity in syllabic number of the word ending each line. Ornament, such as internal rime and alliteration, may be more or less elaborate according to the class of the particular poem; the court poets in their encomiastic verse followed strict rules in this also; in other kinds of verse much variety is found.

SUBJECTS AND AUTHORS

If we consider 'bardic poetry' in its connotation of verse in syllabic metre (*dán díreach*) we are by no means confined to the official poems of the court poets, for encomium and satire do not comprise the whole mass of poetry in this form that has come down to us from the period stretching from the eighth century to the mid-seventeenth. In fact, a fitting title for a general study of early Irish poetry would be 'The place of verse in Irish literature'; because in ancient Ireland —*An Éire bhí anallód ann*—verse was the commonest, one might almost say the common literary medium; not only that, but 'the art' *par excellence*, so that *dán* or *ceard* can be used as a synonym for *filidheacht* in the sense 'poetry'. The man of letters was a poet; if not in all cases an imaginative one, at least a competent versifier, and this tradition was still flourishing in the Munster 'Courts' of the eighteenth century, Daniel Corkery's 'Hidden Ireland'. Even in the nineteenth, some distinguished leaders of the Gaelic revival movement found verse the more natural medium of literary expression since it had been throughout our literary history the more highly cultivated.

Once the strict metres had been adopted they were applied to almost every subject considered worthy of study and literary expression, so we have poems didactic, religious, lyrical, humorous, narrative of various kinds. We have in verse not only native works in history, genealogy, law, toponymy, grammar, theology, but also renderings of Latin and Greek (or at any rate ultimately Greek) treatises on geography, history, biblical exegesis and Latin grammar. In their preference for verse as a general literary medium, the Irish were, of course, following the early Christian tradition of Europe, and to some extent the classical one.[1] But there are indications of a popular liking for prose, and the native tendency may have been towards that. It is noteworthy that the native epic, *Táin Bó Cualnge*, is essentially a prose composition, while the pseudo-historical compilation called *Lebor Gabála* ('Book of Invasions,' or rather 'Occupations'), which reflects a kind of Latin learning, is primarily a metrical one. Biblical history is versified in *Saltair na Rann* ('The psalter of stanzas') and the Irish rendering of the *Sex aetates* is sprinkled with verse paraphrases.

The historical poems in the Book of Invasions, some of which belong to the eleventh century, some to an earlier period, are, when not anonymous or ascribed to mythical persons, admittedly the work of monastic scholars. In introducing the poems, these are referred to by various titles, e.g., *suí senchusa* ('learned in history'), *suí* ('learned man'), *fili* ('poet, learned poet'), *poeta*, *senchaid* ('historian'). The name of the author is sometimes introduced in the concluding stanzas of such poems; Eochu ua Flainn reveals himself in this way in several pieces, e.g., one on the deaths

---

[1] In the introduction to her translation of Dante's *Purgatory* (Penguin Classics) Dorothy Sayers makes some interesting observations on 'the artificial distinction' . . . 'quite unknown in earlier ages' which is nowadays made between 'poetic' and 'prosaic' subjects.

of the leaders of the Milesian invaders (*Book of Leinster* 16ᵃ) introduced by . . . *ro chan in senchaid*,[1] begins:

> Toísig na llongse dar ler
> dia táncatar meic Míled,
> bit mebra limsa rim lá
> a n-anmand 'sa n-aideda.

'The leaders of this fleet overseas when the sons of Míl arrived, I shall remember all my days their names and their violent deaths,' and ends:

> A Christ ós clannaib cuimnig
> mac meic Flaind a laechLuignib,
> a Rí na mblat is na mbreth
> is tú in t-abb is tú in toesech.

'O Christ, above all offspring, remember the grandson of Flann of the warlike Luigni; O King of might and of judgement, Thou art the lord, Thou art the leader.'

LITERARY STYLE

There is one essential fact about Irish poetry which must never be forgotten if we are to appraise it justly: it is, with the possible exception of certain didactic compositions, composed for the ear, and at all periods of its history has been associated with music, the word-music of its own characteristic form and the music of an accompanying instrument. An author's name when it is prefixed to a poem in manuscript is regularly followed by the symbol *.cc.* which originally stood for Latin *cecinit*, but is also used for its Irish cognate and equivalent *ro cechain*. The later form *ro chan*, written in full, is also common.

This delight in the music of words is what gives to Irish poetry its especial aesthetic character. The balance between

---

[1] A glossator here ascribes the poem to Flann Mainistrech, but cf. 6a9, 10b40, 22a30.

30

delight for the ear and satisfaction for the mind may in many official compositions appear to be unevenly held, but we must accept the fact that aural enjoyment was, though not the whole, an integral part of every poem. Each stanza is an aural design.[1] With a skilled and intelligent craftsman this attention to ornament can accompany genuine feeling and even be quickened by it. It need not be a bar to expression and is often a stimulus. The true artist is served by the difficulties of his medium, and the Irish poet, even in his most rigidly patterned quatrains, can express a mood, serious, tender or humorous. There are indeed plenty of dull encomiums consisting of stock epithets fitted into a complex mosaic of sound; but on the other hand a similar intricacy of ornament is often found in convincing expression of genuine emotion, as for instance in Muiredhach Albanach's lament for his dead wife, quoted below, p. 84.

It is worth recalling that Matthew Arnold, who had no first-hand acquaintance with the Celtic languages, found in the translations on which he based his judgment the 'most striking quality' to be 'a sense of style,' and this is undoubtedly an especial characteristic of classical Irish poetry; what the *fili* says is said effectively, pungently, and even banality is invested with dignity.[2]

Of literary style there will be more to say later in this work, where the court poetry is discussed. In early didactic and narrative poems the requirements of the metre combined with the restrictions imposed by the subject entailed occasional artificialities of expression, and chevilles or 'tags' are especially frequent in such compositions. Nowhere perhaps is this wearisome feature more prominent than in the Biblical history called *Saltair na Rann*, composed in the

---

[1] Cf. Robin Flower, in the preface to his *Love's Bitter Sweet*: '. . . the peculiar effect of the Irish manner with its interlacing rimes and balanced phrasing cannot be reproduced in any English which may hope to give the effect of poetry.'

[2] Cf. Flower, *The Irish Tradition*, 110.

the late tenth century[1] in the simplest form of *deibhidhe*, a metre in which the quatrain is composed of two rimed couplets, the riming words being of equal or unequal length according to convenience, and internal rimes optional. The contrast here between the simple and clear style of the actual narrative and the frequent obscurity and at times absurdity of the parenthetical phrases inserted to fill out the verse is very striking. But this poem seems to have been the work of an unpractised hand. No poet could entirely escape the use of such aids, but the really skilful managed to avoid it to a remarkable extent. There are numerous instances where the inserted clauses, though unnecessary for the sense, can be fitted into the context without disturbance:

> Foídis Noe in colum nglan
> uad forin linnmuir n-allmar,
> dús in fagbad, hérimm ngrinn,
> talmain tréin tarbaig tírimm.

'Noah sent the pure dove out on the vast spreading sea, to see if it might find—pleasant course—strong, useful dry land.'

But in the following the words seem less happily chosen:

> Lucifer: Rádimse fri Dia as mo thas
> athesc feochair fíramnas:
> nach hé Ádam, hérim nglé,
> óssar na ndúle n-uile?

'I utter to God out of my silence a fierce stern reply: is not Adam, bright course, the youngest of all creatures?'

There are many stock phrases, nominal and verbal, used generally by the early poets in this way. A simpler device for filling out a line is the addition of adjectives, and this is naturally very common at all periods.

I shall now quote a passage exemplifying the simple

---

[1] Attributed in the earliest known copy to Oengus Céle Dé, who is apparently not to be confounded with the author of the *Félire* or Martyrology cited below.

narrative style of which the poet of SR was capable: David
proclaims his intention to challenge Goliath:

> Regatsa, ar Dauíd cen lén,
> co Saul ríg nIsrahél,
> co tuc a ingin cen clith
> is coro marb in córaid.
>
> Gabsat a charait cech cruth
> a chosc is a chairigud;
> dia bráithrib robo gábud
> a labrad nó a imrádud.
>
> Ro ráidi Dauíd co trén
> fiad dagdaíneib Israhél:
> dingébsa in fer hút don tslóg,
> is tabar dam a daglóg.
>
> Rogellai Saul iar sain
> do Dauíd, cen imresain,
> a ingen dó, demin scél,
> a grád sech clainn nIsrahél.
>
> Ainige fris, fo glóir glain,
> a meic Cis chóir comramaig,
> cen dímiad im choible cruth,
> co fírian dia fírugud.

'I shall go, said David without sorrow, to Saul king of Israel,
that I may take his daughter openly and slay the champion. His
friends in every way fell to restraining him, to chiding him;
to his brethren it was perilous for him to speak of it or think of it.
David said stoutly before the nobles of Israel: I shall ward off
yon man from the host and be the good prize for it given to me.
Saul then promised to David without dispute that he should have
his daughter, sure tidings, his beloved beyond all others of the
Children of Israel. Guarantees for it, under bright fame, O son of
Cis, just, triumphant, without dishonour in ways of hospitality,
for truthfully fulfilling it.'

Some of the historical poems in the Book of Invasions,
referred to above, are in the same simple form of *deibhidhe*

as used in SR; some are in elaborate forms of *rannaigheacht*, etc., with plenty of rime and alliteration, though not so strictly regulated as in the later court poetry. Chevilles are, of course, frequent.

No elaboration of sound-patterns can make exciting for the modern mind what is often little more than a list of proper names mortised into the verse by chevilles or unnecessary and irrelevant adjectives, but occasionally in other documents we come upon a more attractive treatment of some of the LG material. Fintan, son of Bóchra, whose antediluvian origin made him an indispensable witness in matters of prehistory, is quoted fairly often in LG and other pseudo-historical texts, but for light reading his *ipsissima verba* are more favourably presented in the somewhat humorously conceived Dialogue between Fintan and the Hawk of Achill, about fifty stanzas in simple *deibhidhe*. Having met and ascertained that they are both the same age, and indeed have unknowingly encountered one another on previous occasions, these interlocutors proceed to exchange information about their respective adventures in Ireland from the period before the Flood down to Christian times, incidentally including an account of the prehistoric occupations, reference to kings and battles, and a list of river-names, also a certain amount of less prosaic matter. The date of the composition is uncertain; the language does not suggest that it is earlier than the fourteenth century, and it is certainly not later than the mid-fifteenth. It is anonymous. The basic motif is, of course, the folklore one so favoured in Irish legend of the long-lived animal. A transcription of the text is published by Meyer in *Anecdota from Irish Mss*, i, 24 f. I quote some stanzas in translation:[1]

1   Fintan:

That is ancient, O Bird of Achill; tell us the cause of thy journey; I can converse with thee expertly in bird-language.

[1] There is a complete translation by Eleanor Hull in *Folklore*, xliii (1932).

II   The Bird:

As for thee, thy body is not young; it is long since it shrivelled in Dún Tulcha by the sea, O Fintan, thou learned man.

III–IV   Fintan:

More strange is it that I should be living; gloom has settled on my heart; the sorrow of Ros Gredha has maimed me; the tragic death of Illann has grieved me even more. O Bird from Achill of the hunters, I have ever been seeking to behold thee, now that I see thee, tell me why dost thou cling to Achill?

V–VI   The Bird:

The brightness of its sky, the beauty of its harbours, the warmth of its never chill woods, the fruitfulness of its chase, the freedom of its streams and the quiet solitude of its bays. O Fintan, I was never a night in Achill to the west that I could not get by my skill all I could devour of fish, of game, of venison.

VIII–X   Fintan:

Fifteen years was my life before the dark Flood and after it God gave me five thousand and five hundred. More again did I get, O Bird, that is the reason of my aged plight, ten hundred years, enough to make me old. O Hawk from cold Achill, bear a blessing and success; from the day thou camest forth from an egg, say the number of thy days?

XI–XII   The Bird:

Our days are the same, O Fintan son of generous Bóchra, precisely the same age, no treacherous matter; equal our goodly age since the Flood. O Fintan son of white Bóchra, since thou art seer and prophet, tell us now without delay the greatest ills thou hast suffered.

XIII–XIV; XVIII–XXI   Fintan:

The loss of Illann, the destruction of my sons, the death of Cessair of the white hands; more again was I tormented by my night on seal-haunted Eas Ruaidh [Assaroe]. After the loss of Ladra and pleasant Bioth, after the dark pouring of the Flood, the Lord to my sorrow put me in the guise of a salmon on every chill stream [he then recites the names of the principal rivers of Ireland, all frequented by him in salmon shape, until:] One night I was on the wave in the north, on seal-haunted Eas Ruaidh; such a night I never found in all my time. I could not remain beneath the falls; I made a leap and it was not for my good; the ice like blue crystal came between me and the Falls of Modharn's son. There came a crow from cold Achill over the river-mouth at Eas Ruaidh. I will not hide it though it be a mystery, he robbed me of one eye. Goll (the one-eyed) of Eas Ruaidh has stuck to me (as a name) ever since that night; I am since that without the eye, cause enough to make me old.

The Bird:

It was I, the gray hawk that dwells alone in the bosom of Achill, who swallowed thine eye, O Fintan . . .

Fintan:

If thou art he, thou didst leave me, though it is perverse, gloomy and blind; pay me, it is lawful and natural, the eric of mine eye.

The Bird:

I will give thee a little eric, O Fintan son of generous Bóchra; that eye that is in thy head I will swallow it readily in one morsel.

Fintan:

Bitter is what thou singest, thou great crazy bird . . . I, since I am gentler than thou, will converse with thee about my coevals.

And so he proceeds with an account of his adventures during his various metamorphoses, and the Bird rejoins with a grim list of his own trophies from battlefields through the ages, and of successful raids for game and domestic cattle, the whole forming a curious compendium in pleasant verse of what is sometimes called 'Bardic history'.

ANONYMITY

Our early imaginative poetry, both religious and other, has one feature which clearly marks it off from the court poetry of the period 1200–1650; it is almost completely anonymous. When an author's name is prefixed to a poem it is usually uncertain whether or no the ascription is even intended to be taken seriously. There are nearly two hundred poems in Irish ascribed in our manuscripts to Colum Cille, of which it is unbelievable that he composed even one. We have some pleasing ones ascribed to the saint Mo Lling which are certainly hundreds of years later than the time in which he is said to have lived. They form the metrical portions of a Mo Lling saga, of which the *Bóroma*, the history of the tribute exacted periodically from Leinster by the kings of Tara, includes the first part. In fact the most delightful of the early lyrics occur in prose texts.[1] The prose narrative or treatise interspersed with verse, though common enough in the Christian Latin literature of Europe from Boëthius on, seems a comparatively late form in Irish. In some examples the prose seems rather to connect the lengthy metrical passages. Few of the longer tales of the later period are without versified passages, but they are not usual in early texts. Verse, significantly, is not characteristic of the earlier portions of the Ulster cycle; it is conspicuously absent from the more primitive tales such as the Siege of Étar, though there is a brief metrical dialogue in *Scél Mucce Maic dá Thó*. There is no verse in the surviving fragments of *Táin Bó Fraích*, but in the later Fraech story, *Tochmarc Trebhlainne*, it is freely used. The early redaction of *Táin Bó Cualnge* has a few short metrical passages, some of them certainly later interpolations. More noteworthy in this text are the 'rhetorics', passages of rhythmical speech or dialogue in very archaic language, which frequently interrupt the course of the narrative (without, for modern

[1] Anonymous, of course.

37

readers, elucidating either what precedes or what follows). These are introduced by *ut dixit* (*Ailill, Medb, Fergus,* etc.) or *co cloth ní, co cloth* (*Ailill,* etc.): 'Something was heard, (Ailill, saying).' Such passages may retain genuinely older strata of the legend, or they may be artificial insertions. For their style Thurneysen compares the later Latin rhetorical style especially as used by Irish latinists in such compositions as the *Hisperica Famina*.[1] *Fled Bricrend,* which has no strict verse, has also several rhetorics, but of a later style than those in the *Táin. Togal Bruidne Da Derga* in the early redaction has a few very archaic rhetorical passages, but of strict verse only one couplet; *Longas Mac nUislenn* has a long rhetorical passage as well as a dialogue and lament in *deibhidhe.* The story of the combat of Cú Chulainn and Fer diad, as it has come down to us, is later than the preceding portions of the Táin, and the graceful lyrics in *ochtfhoclach* which adorn it emphasise the distinct style of this episode. The language, as Thurneysen says (*Heldensage,* p. 219), points to the eleventh century; whether he is right in holding that the metre used precludes an earlier date is not so certain, but cf. Windisch's edition of *Táin Bó Cualnge,* p. 434.

EARLY RELIGIOUS POETRY

The early religious verse is mainly lyrical and contemplative. It has spontaneity and freshness of expression as well as an easy grace of form. As a whole it reflects clearly the ascetic and mystical yet deeply charitable character of early Irish Christianity. Especially frequent are poems which express the craving of the religious for solitude, to be alone with God and nature, and to rejoice in a life of innocence and repentance. Here are a few stanzas from one of these;[2] the metre is a favourite one for poems of this class, the odd lines are

[1] *Heldensage,* p. 12.

[2] There is a complete edition of this poem, with translation, by Gerard Murphy in his *Early Irish Lyrics* (Oxford, 1956).

seven-syllabled, ending in a trisyllable; the even are five-syllabled, ending in a monosyllable. The rime of the even lines is strict, that of the odd optional, often imperfect. The name of the metre is *cró cumaisc eder casbhairdne 7 leathrannaigheacht mhóir*.[1]

M'aenurán im aireglán
cen duinén im gnáis;
robo inmain ailithrán
ria ndul i ndáil báis.

Bothán derrit diämair
do dílgud gach cloín;
cubus dírech diämain
dochum nime noíb.

Noíbad cuirp co sobésaib,
slatrad ferda for,
súilib tláithib todéraib
do dílgud mo thol.

. . .

Céim iar sétaib soscéla,
salmchetal cach tráth;
crích fri rád, fri roscéla,
filliud glúine gnáth.

Mo Dúilem dom thathigi
mo Choimdiu, mo Rí;
mo menma dia athigi
sin mbithflaith i mbí.

. . .

M'aenurán im airiclán,
m'aenurán im-ne;
m'aenur do-lod forsin mbith,
m'aenur ragad de.

[1] In my citations here and below I usually follow the spelling of the manuscript or printed text quoted.

'Alone in my little cell without anyone in my company, beloved to me were that pilgrimage before going to meet death. A hidden remote little dwelling for the absolving of every iniquity, a sincere faultless conscience towards holy heaven. To sanctify the body by good habits, stoutly subduing it; with tender weeping eyes to dissolve my passions . . . Stepping along the paths of the gospel; chanting of psalms at prayer-times, an end to talk, to story-telling; genuflexion continually . . . My Creator to visit me, my Lord, my King; my mind attentive to Him, in the enduring kingdom wherein He dwelleth . . . Alone in my little cell, alone like this; alone I came into the world, alone I shall go from it.'

And here are two stanzas from a Metrical Rule. The language points to the eighth century. The metre varies from time to time, but the main one is *rannaigheacht bheag*, seven-syllabled lines, each ending in a disyllable; the even lines rime; internal rime occurs occasionally:

> Is ed as dech na riaglae
> car Críst, miscnigthe moíni;
> lére duit fri Ríg ngréne
> ocus réde fri doíni.
> Nírba chreccach cundarthach,
> do Chríst ba mór do gaire;
> ní foigis ríg i nÉre
> dia mba chéle Maicc Maire.

(The third line of the last stanza quoted should, like the others, have short vowels in the end-word; the lapse here is compensated by the *aicill-* rime with *chéle* in the fourth.)

'This is the best of the Rule: Love Christ, hate riches; use diligence towards the King of the sun; use gentleness towards men . . . Practise not buying or bargaining; great be thy piety to Christ; thou shouldst not appeal to any king in Erin if thou beest a vassal of the Son of Mary [i.e. a *Céle Dé*, 'Culdee'].'

The following verses are in praise of St. Fionnbharr. The last line refers to his descent from Brion son of Echu

40

Muigmedón. They probably belong to the tenth century. The metre is of the class called *echraid* (or *echred*) which includes several species. Here the stanzas are linked by the riming of the final lines; there is no rime within the stanza. Alliteration is lacking in only one line. The epithet *breó* 'flame' is a favourite one in such poems; *Brigit bé bithmaith, breó órda oíblech* 'Brigid, woman ever good, golden sparkling flame' is the opening of Ultan's hymn.

> Bairre breó bithbuadach
> buaid betha brethadbuil
> ruithen réil rathamra
> ruithniges Ébermag
> lia luagmar lainnerda
> ní luad nach liúin.
>
> Eó órda ilchrothach
> uaisliu cach caínchumdach
> aire ard ollairbrech
> ernes cach n-olladlaic
> do buidnib balcBanba
> barr Brogha Briúin.[1]

'Bairre, ever-triumphant flame, victory of the vast-bearing world; clear ray of wondrous grace that lightens the Plain of Eber; a glistening precious stone, it is not the lauding of any sluggard. A golden multiform brooch, nobler than any smooth ornament; high lord of many hosts who endows all the needy ones of the bands of firm Banba; glory of the land of Brion.'

The following stanzas are from a Litany of the Blessed Virgin, ascribed in some manuscripts to Colum Cille, but hardly early enough for his authorship. The symbolism, deriving from the Canticles, Isaiah and other books of the Old Testament, recalls that used in the twelfth-century sequences, and by St. Bernard. The text here is from Laud 615. A complete edition from all the manuscripts, with translation, is given by G. Murphy, *loc. cit.*

---

[1] Bairre breó . . .: see *Irische Texte*, iii, p. 57.

A Maire mín maithingen
   tabair furtacht dún;
a chriol chuirp choimdeta,
   a chomrair na rún.

A rígain na rígraide,
   a noíbingen óg,
áil dam cora dílgaithe
   triut ar tairmthecht tróg.

. . .

A chróeb do chlainn Iësse
   isin chollchaill choím,
áil dom conom biësse
   dílgad mo chuil chloín.

A Maire, a mind mórmaisech,
   ro shaorais ar síl,
a lésbaire lórmaisech,
   a lubgort na ríg.

. . .

A rígdorus rogaide
   trisar chin i crí
grian taitnemach togaide,
   Ísu Mac Dé bí.

'O Mary, gentle tender maid, give help to us; O casket of the Lord's Body, O coffer of the mysteries. O queen of all royalties, O holy virgin maid, beseech for us that through thee our piteous transgressions be forgiven. O branch of the plant of Jesse from the fair hazel-wood, beseech for me that I may have forgiveness for my wicked sin. O Mary, O comely diadem, thou didst deliver our race, O most comely torch, O herb-garden of kings . . . O royal chosen gateway through whom there entered into flesh the shining choice Sun, Jesus Son of the living God!'

Before leaving this part of our subject, I should like to quote from the eighth-century Martyrology of Oengus, *Félire Oengusso*, these grave and stately verses on the transience of human greatness as typified by events in the poet's own land. The metre is *rionnard*, of which the principal requisites are six-syllabled lines ending in disyllables with even lines riming:

Cid a tír i taam
ata saidbri saigthe,
di neurt Dé, deilm sochlae
fil and dún ro praidche.

At-bath borg tromm Temra
le tairthim a flathe;
co llín corad sruthe
maraid Ard mór Machae.

Ro múchad, mór tairbaid,
miad Loíguire roglaig;
ainm Pátraic án aurdairc
atá som for forbairt.

Fororbart in chretem,
méraid co dé mbrátha,
genti bidbaid bertar,
ní trebtar a rrátha.

Ráth Chrúachan ro scáichi
la hAilill, gein mbúada;
caín ordan úas flathib
fil i cathir Chlúana.

. . .

Borg Ailline úallach
at-bath lia slóg bágach,
is mór Brigit búadach,
is caín a rrúam dálach.

Borg Emna ro tetha
acht mairte a clocha,
is rúam iarthair betha
Glenn dálach dá locha.

43

In the following rendering the metre of the original is imitated as regards syllabic system and rime, but the rimes are merely vowel-rimes without the strict consonantal correspondence used in the Irish; and alliteration is ignored. In a few cases I have had to strain the meaning of a word *metri gratia*. In the second line of the first stanza here both text and translation are uncertain.

E'en in this our country,
    whose riches thou seekest,
of God's might, sound famous,
    is something can teach us.

No more lives strong Tara,
    her lordships are blighted;
with full choirs of preachers
    Armagh is still mighty.

Stifled—great prevention—
    the pride of brave Laere;
But Patrick's fame brightly
    still increaseth daily.

Here the Faith hath flourished,
    till doom it shall prosper;
the pagans are routed,
    their raths remain cropless.

Rath Croghan lies ruined,
    with Ailill the gifted;
state beyond all sovrans
    lives in Cluain's city.

    . . .

The proud burgh of Allen
    is gone, and its armies;
triumphant is Brigid,
    fair her Rome's thronged arches.

Strong Emain hath vanished,
    only stones remaining;
Rome of the world westward,
    Glendaloch stands famous.

LOVE POEMS

Only a small number of love-poems have come down to us from the Old- and Middle-Irish period, and these are attributed to women. There is the lament of Créde, daughter of Guaire, for Dínertach, translated in Meyer's *Selections* and in G. Murphy's *Early Irish Lyrics*; Deirdre's lament for the Sons of Uisnech, of which we possess an Old-Irish version (unfortunately in a corrupt text) as well as an Early-modern one well preserved in a fifteenth-century vellum; there is the famous Liadain and Cuirithir poem (fragmentary, alas!) cited in the early metrical tracts as a specimen of *treochair* metre:

> Cen áinius
> in caingen do-rigénus;
> nech ro charus ro cráidius.

'Joyless the bargain I made; him whom I loved I have tortured.'

In *Agallamh na Senórach*, a very moving and poetical lament for a warrior drowned after the battle of Ventry is given to another Créde, daughter of Cairbre. I quote a few stanzas:

> Géisid cuan
> ós buinne ruad Rinn dá bhárc
> bádud laeich Locha dá chonn
> is ed chaínes tonn re trácht.

> . . .

> Truag in faíd
> do-ní in smólach i nDruim chaín,
> ocus ní nemthruaige in scol
> do-ní in lon i Leitir laeigh.

> . . .

> Truag in gháir
> do-ní tonn tráchta re tráig,
> ó do báid fer segda saer
> saeth lem Cael do dul na dáil.

45

Truag in fuaimm
do-ní in tonn risin trácht tuaid;
ag cenngail um charraic chaín
ag caíned Chaeil ó do-chuaid.

I quote O'Grady's rendering, omitting his needless repetition of the first line of each stanza:

'The haven roars over the rushing race of Rinn dá bharc! the drowning of the warrior of Loch dá chonn, that is what the wave impinging on the strand laments . . . A woeful note is that which the thrush in Drumqueen emits! but not more cheerful is the wail the blackbird makes in Letterlee . . . A dismal roar is that the shore's surf makes upon the strand! seeing that the same hath drowned the comely noble man, to me it is an affliction that ever Cael sought to encounter it. A woeful booming is that which the wave makes upon the northward beach! butting as it does against the polished rock, lamenting for Cael now that he has gone.'

With the exception of the first mentioned, all these love poems occur in prose texts, and even the first, though only found appended to some anecdotes about Guaire, is probably part of a (now lost) saga on the battle of Aidhne. Poetry gathered round this daughter of Guaire, she is the heroine of the most poetic of our early tales that have survived, the story of Cano son of Gartnán, which contains the Irish tradition of the Tristan legend. There is only one copy, and unfortunately the text, both prose and verse is corrupt in several places.

The later love poems, the *dánta grádha* collected and edited by T. F. O'Rahilly,[1] are of a special kind. In his brilliant introduction[2] contributed to O'Rahilly's book, Robin Flower has fully analysed their nature and quality, and this essay must be studied by those who wish to appreciate fully this facet of our literature.

[1] *Dánta Grádha*, an anthology of Irish love-poetry . . . (second edition 1926).

[2] Partly reprinted in the posthumous volume of Flower's essays, *The Irish Tradition* (Oxford, 1947).

The love these poems celebrate, according to Flower, is not 'the direct passion of the folksingers, or the high vision of the great poets, but . . . the *amour courtois*, which was first shaped into art for modern Europe in Provence. . . .'

This poetry is, as Flower puts it, 'clearly the poetry of society'. Not all the authors named (most of the poems are anonymous in the manuscripts) were professional poets; the earliest of them is, significantly, Gearóid Iarla, also called Gerald the Rymer, that famous Earl of Desmond, chief justice of Ireland in 1367, who was not only a 'rymer' himself, but a generous patron of the Irish poets. Five poems are attributed to a scion of the native Irish nobility, Maghnas Ó Domhnaill. Whether this Maghnas was, as Flower supposed, chief of his clan, is not so certain.

None of the poems in the collection can be dated earlier than the mid-fourteenth century, and many, perhaps the majority, are more than two centuries later. It is possible however, that earlier examples were extant and have perished.

It is not to be supposed that we are presented here with a dull monotony of expression, a tedious repetition of identical complaints. In fact, though the subject is one, the paths of approach are remarkably varied. Further, as Flower himself emphasizes, despite the apparently exotic tone in many of these poems, the native Irish flavour is not lost. Because of the variety of expression—the poet may be cheerful, mournful, whimsical, cynical.[1] His theme may be the loved one's beauty, her indifference, her folly (or his own). Or philosophizing on the nature of love, its joy, its madness, its sorrow, its torment, its perils. One would need to quote very extensively to give a just notion of the varied character of the collection. I quote here not any complete poem, but a small selection of stanzas.

We have seen that in Irish classical poetry (as in the poetry

---

[1] A small number of examples in the manuscripts show that he could also be, on occasion, extremely indecorous, in quite a stately style.

47

of the troubadours), form is of prime importance, and the discipline of form goes with a dignity of style which can all too easily be lost in translation. In these poems the fully elaborate system of rime and alliteration used in the official court poetry is rare, but the simpler forms used are strictly followed. In my versions here I cannot be confident that I have always completely conveyed the subtlety of meaning, or the tone of the originals. I have followed in nearly every line the syllabic quantity of the originals; my rimes are merely vowel-rimes, the Irish are usually, not invariably, consonantal also. What I have tried to do is to give as far as possible a literal rendering of the words set in a close imitation of the metre. I trust that this may enable even the novice to follow with some appreciation the original text.[1] In the references to *Dánta Grádha* at the end of each quotation the number of stanzas in the complete poem is given in square brackets.

Courtly love is usually love of the absent, even the unobtainable. It may be covert:

> Ní truagh galar acht gradh falaigh,—
>   uch, is fada gur smuain mé;
> ní bhiad níos sia gan a nochtadh,
>   mo ghrádh folaigh don tseing shéimh
>
> Tugas grádh nach féadaim d'fholach
>   dá folt cochlach, dá rún leasg,
> dá malainn chaoil, dá rosg (gormghlas),
>   dá déid shocair, dá gnúis tais.
>
> Tugas fós, gion go n-admhann,
>   grádh mar mh'anam dá píp réidh,
> dá guth roibhinn, dá béal blasta,
>   dá hucht sneachtmhar, dá cíghghéir.

---

[1] For fine translations of some complete poems see Robin Flower's *Love's Bitter Sweet*, the Earl of Longford's *Poems from the Irish* 1949, *More Poems from the Irish* 1955, Frank O'Connor's *Kings, Lords and Commons* 1959.

'Love that's veiled is sorest sickness,
  long I've pondered that, my grief;
I'll no more defer unveiling
  my love for the graceful queen.

Love I gave, there's no concealing,
  to her curled locks, her shy mind,
her pencilled brows, grey eyes glancing,
  her trim teeth, her aspect mild.

I gave also, though unuttered,
  my soul's love to her smooth throat,
to her sweet voice, her speech graceful,
  her breast shapely, white as snow . . .'

(*DG*24 [5§§], *lines* 1–12.)

Maghnas Ó Domhnaill chants with playful sadness on the
theme of the lover's heart:

. . . Uaimse ag inghin an iarla
  Truagh gan iasacht mo chroidhe,
go dtuigeadh féin nách bhféadar
  bréagadh croidhe i mbí toirse.

Cuirfead iomchar mo chroidhe
  ar dhuine oile i mbliadhna;
gidh eadh, dá gcleachta a iomchar,
  biaidh sí diomdhach don iasacht.

Biaidh sí tinn, biaidh sí corrach,
  biaidh sí gan chodladh choidhche;
biaidh sí ciamhair cumhach,
  biaidh sí dubhach gach n-oidhche.

Ni iarrfa adhbhar gáire,
  badh sáimhe lé bheith dubhach,
go sgara sí rem chroidhe
  go bráth ní bhfoighe furtacht.

Uch! Ní cothrom an roinnse
  do-ní an toirrse, dar linne,—
croidhe nó dhó ag duine,
  is duine oile gan chridhe!

49

'. . . Would that the earl's fair daughter
   had sought my heart to borrow,[1]
that she might learn 'tis bootless
   to soothe[2] a heart in sorrow.

My heart this year I'll offer
   to another one to carry,
but, if she bear it daily,
   the loan won't make her happy.

She shall be sick and restless,
   she shall be ever sleepless;
she shall be sad and woeful,
   and doleful every even.

She will not seek amusement,
   gloom she will deem more pleasant;
till our two hearts be sundered
   ne'er shall she learn contentment.

Unfair, alas, the sharing
   that sorrow makes for lovers:[3]
two hearts with but one owner,
   and no heart with another.'

                (*DG* 49 [6§§], *ll.* 5-24).

Some poets argue the claims of death:

Do cuireadh bréag ar an mbás,
   ní mar deirthear atá a ghoimh;
díol a loisgthe lucht na mbréag;
   mairg do chreidfeadh a sgéal soin.

A tharbha dá dtuigeadh neach
   a urghráin is beag an cás;
fa ríor is amadán bocht
   do-gheabhadh locht ar an mbás.

---

[1] *Lit.* sad that the earl's daughter has not my heart from me on loan.
[2] *Lit.* beguile.   [3] *Lit.* that sorrow makes, meseems.

Éagóir adubhradh ris riamh;
    an lá is measa bhias do chách,
dar ndóigh, a dhuine gan chéill,
    is cairdeamhla é ná an grádh . . .

'Death hath had a false report,
    Its torture is not so keen;
the deceivers should be burned,
    woe him whom their words mislead.

Its profit did each man know,
    its loathsomeness were small fret;
Ah, he's but a wretch distraught,
    whoso findeth fault with death.

Wrongly hath it aye been famed,
    the worst day it ever come,
true it is, O witless men:
    death is friendlier than love . . .'

              (*DG* 35 [14§§], *ll.* 1–12.)

Another dismisses this solution with contempt:

Ní bhfuighe mise bás duit,
    a bhean úd an chuirp mar ghéis;
daoine leamha ar mharbhais riamh,
    ní hionann iad is mé féin.

Créad umá rachainnse d'éag
    don bhéal dearg, don déad mar bhláth?
an crobh míolla, an t-ucht mar aol,
    an dáibh do-gheabhainn féin bás?

Do mhéin aobhdha, th'aigneadh saor,
    a bhas thana, a thaobh mar chuip,
a rosg gorm, a bhrágha bhán,
    ní bhfuighe mise bás duit.

'I shall not die for thy sake,
    O maid with the swan-like grace,
Dull wights all whom thou hast slain
    I am not the same as they.

Wherefore should I go to death
  for red lips, for gleaming teeth?
The soft hand, the bosom white,
  Should I give my life for these?

Thy pleasant mien, thy high mind,
  Thy slim hand, O foam-white maid,[1]
O blue eye, O bosom white,
  I shall not die for thy sake . . .'

             (*DG* 99 [6§§], *ll.* 1–12.)

'Love aislings [i.e., visions of beautiful women] are,' to quote Gerard Murphy,[2] 'old, and occur at every stage of Irish literature.' There are a few included in *Dánta Grádha*, the one from which I quote, is not manifestly a dream story, but is certainly one of the familiar Irish vision type. It is by Maghnas Ó Domhnaill:

Cia thú, a mhacaoimh mná?
  créad is fáth dod chuairt?
Uch! is géar rom chráidh,
  más triall dob áil duit uaim.

Síth Lir, searc gach súl,
  an í súd do threabh?
Nó Sídh Buidhbh na mbuadh?
  Uch, mo nuar! a bhean . . .

Ní hiongnadh, a dhreach mhín,
  gibé chí do chruth
baintsíodh riot do rádh,
  a ghnúis mar bhláth subh.

Ní dearg deirge an ghuail
  i ngar dod ghruaidh ghil;
do dhorchaigh gné an aoil
  bheith re taobh do chnis . . .

---

[1] *Lit.* side like foam.
[2] In his valuable paper, entitled 'Notes on Aisling Poetry', *Éigse*, i, 40 ff.

Mo bhruidse an truagh lat?
   fogas damh an bás;
mairg nách admhann dún
   cia thú a mhacaoimh mná!

'Lady, who art thou?
   wherefore dost thou roam?
Ah, it pricks me sore
   if thou wouldst be gone.

Síth Lir, all eyes' delight,
   is that thy dwelling-place?
Or Bov's famed abode,
   ochone, my fair dame? . . .

No wonder, smooth face,
   whoso sees thy looks
names thee fairy maid,
   cheek like berry's bloom . . .

Not red the hot coal
   beside thy fair cheek;
darkened is the lime
   near thy bright skin's gleam . . .

Dost thou pity me?
   death is near me now;
woe that none will say
   Lady, who art thou?'

     (*DG* 48 [8§§], *ll.* 1–8, 17–24, 29–32.)

Less artificial in tone than the above is a dramatic poem
by Niall Mhac Mhuireadhaigh:

. . . Atáid dias is tighse anocht
   ar nach ceileann rosg a rún;
gion go bhfuilid béal re béal,
   is géar géar silleadh a súl.

Tocht an ní chuireas an chiall
   ar shilleadh siubhlach na súl;
cá feirrde an tocht do-ní an béal
   sgéal do-ní an rosg ar a rún?

53

Uch, ní léigid lucht na mbréag
  smid tar mo bhéal, a rosg mall;
tuig an níse adeir mo shúil
  agus tú insan chúil úd thall . . .

'. . . Two there are within to-night
  whose eyes do not hide their hearts;
though they meet not with their lips,
  swift are their eyes, and sharp.

Silence 'tis that gives a sense
  to the eyes' unresting march;
what boots it if lips refrain,
  while the eyes betray the heart?

The liars will not let, alas,
  my lips to part, O slow look;[1]
take my meaning from my eyes,
  while thou stayst in yonder nook . . .'

(*DG* 38 [6§§], 5–16.)

Poetry of the kind we have been considering in the last few chapters, lyrical, imaginative, occasional, has not been so carefully preserved as other, less interesting kinds. Some examples are merely quoted in metrical tracts, or glossaries; incompletely, of course; some, as I have said, occur in prose narratives; others again merely as scribal marginalia. There is little doubt that much treasure has been lost, thrown away as ballast by tasteless scribes.

OSSIANIC POEMS[2]

Finally, it must not be forgotten that larger in bulk in our literary heritage even than the copious court poetry is the

---

[1] *Lit.* slow eye. I have translated the adjective literally, as that may best preserve the poet's meaning here; but *rosg* (*súil*) *m.* is one of the commonest epithets in the official ecomiums, and in this use *mall* is usually rendered by 'stately', 'gentle', 'grave', or some such word.

[2] For a detailed and comprehensive study of the Ossianic tradition see G. Murphy's *Duanaire Finn*, iii (Ir. Texts Soc. xliii).

almost completely anonymous 'Ossianic' or 'Fenian' descriptive and narrative verse, nature poems, tales of love and courtship, the chase and battle; these also belong in origin to the *dán díreach* style,[1] as copies of many in good manuscripts from the twelfth century on amply witness, although the great popularity of this verse, which has perpetuated so much of it through the corrupting medium of oral narration, has tended to obscure the fact. *Agallamh na Senórach*, 'The conversation of the old men', from which the lines from Créde's lament are quoted above, belongs of course to the Ossianic corpus.[2] It is the record of the reminiscences of Oisín and Caoilte in their old age, of their courtings, their hunts and their battles; of buried treasure, of elfmounds, werewolves and other wonders; it is in form the Irish equivalent of 'the Arabian nights', a collection of stories enframed in a story, told, however, not to a jealous sultan, but written down, we are informed, at the instance of Patrick's guardian angel, to be 'a pastime to the companies and nobles of the latest times'. Whitley Stokes, who edited the longer version in 1900, comments on the sadness of the non-fulfilment of this prophecy: 'In Ireland at least, there are now few companies and no nobles that are able to read them.' Some of the most widely known of our nature poems are in the *Agallamh*, such as that on Arran (in the Clyde), as well as others equally pleasing if less familiar.[3]

These poems bring us nostalgic memories of a perished golden age. The dialogues of Oisín and Patrick, apparently a rather late composition, at least show what capabilities of development this branch held in comparison with the court poetry. The Ossianic poems appealed to all: they spread throughout Ireland and were carried to the highlands of

---

[1] Not of course to the strictly elaborate style of the court poetry.

[2] *Agallamh na Senórach* is cited from the edition by Whitley Stokes, *Irische Texte*, iv.

[3] See Flower, *The Irish Tradition*, 101 f.

Scotland, whence they were destined to infuse a new spirit into European literature.

In illustration of the style, I shall quote from *Duanaire Finn* some stanzas of Oisín's mournful musings:

> A bhen, dén folcadh mo chinn,
> cian ó do sgar re féin Finn;
> bliadhain ar chóig, mór an modh,
> nach ffuair aoinbhen dia fholcadh.

> Sé bliadhna dég gus anocht
> aoibhinn damhsa fóm dheghfholt,
> doiligh aithne in chinn sin de
> tar éis trillsi thonnbhuidhe.

> Uchán: fa hé in cenn truagh
> fá ndéndís conart conuall;
> dámadh an lá ar Leitir Lon,
> do-gheubhadh mná dá fholcadh.

> A thurus co Leitir Lon,
> turus fár ghnáth mór ccoscar,
> dár mharbhsamar daimh dhonna
> ós ur Locha Liathdroma.

'O woman, wash my head: It is long since it parted with Finn's company; for six years, great the deed, it has found no woman to wash it. Sixteen years till to-night, happy was I then 'neath my noble locks; hard afterwards to recognise that head bereft of its yellow tresses. Alas! It was a sorrowful head around which dogs would bay; if it were the day on Leitir Lon it would find women to wash it. Its trip to Leitir Lon, a trip from which much triumph was usual, when we slew the brown deer above the shore of Loch Liathdroma . . .'

And, again from the *Agallamh*:

> Is fuar geimred, atracht gaeth,
> éirgid dam díscir dergbaeth;
> ní te anocht in sliab slán
> gé beth dam dian ic dordán.

56

Ní thabair a thaeb re lár
dam shléibe Cairnn na comdál,
ní luga at-chluin ceól cuaine
dam Chinn Echtge innuaire.

Missi, ar Caílte, is Diarmaid donn,
ocus Oscar áith étrom,
ro chloistmís re ceól cuaine
dered aidche adfhuaire.

As maith chodlus in dam donn
fuil is a chnes re Coronn,
mar do beth fa Tuinn Tuaidhi
dered aidche innuaire.

Aniu isam senóir sen,
ní aithnim acht becán fer;
ro chraithinn coirrshleig co cruaid
a maduin oigrid innuair,

At-lochar do Ríg nime,
do Mhac Muire ingine,
do-berinn mór socht ar sluag,
gé beor anocht co hadfhuar.

'Cold is the winter, the wind has risen; the restless frantic stag goes up; not warm at night is the safe moorland, though the swift stag is belling. The stag from the mount of Carn na comdál does not lie down, neither does the stag of chill Aughty fail to hear the music of the wolf-pack. I, says Caoilte, and brown Dermot and swift, light-footed Oscar used to listen to the wolves' strain at the end of a keenly cold night. Soundly sleeps the brown stag that nestles against Corann as though he were neath Tonn Tuaige at the end of a chill cold night. To-day I am an old ancient man; few men do I know. I was wont to brandish a sharp spear on an icy cold morn. I give thanks to the King of heaven, to the Son of the maiden Mary, I used to silence a whole host, though I be full cold this night.'

But Fionn's men were not always exposed to the icy darts of winter, on the cold hill-side; a poem in *Duanaire Finn*

recounts the warm cheer which awaited the warriors returning laden from the chase: women decked with golden brace-
lets dispensing intoxicating mead from vats of yew-wood
into drinking vessels of gold and silver; lofty candle-sticks
of the same metals; beds and recesses of wood and wattle
with gilt pillars, etc. All this they found in Fionn's house at
Almu, of which now not a stick remains; 'the deserted site
is grassy and green-surfaced'.

The dialogue poems are of especial interest. The exchanges between Oisín and Patrick have a humorous tone,
but there are also more serious and more dramatic dialogues,
such as that between the warrior Goll and his wife, in which,
beset by foes and hemmed in on a rocky promontory with
his back to sea, he tells her to leave him and take refuge with
his enemies. I quote a few stanzas in translation; for the
whole poem see *Duanaire Finn* i, edited by Eóin MacNéill,
Irish Texts Soc., vii, p. 23 f.:

'O woman, take my tunic and depart from me; make the
attempt, in the morn, before I am slain.

O Goll, what path shall I take? Alas for those whose
friends are few; rarely has a woman any fortune who is without
head or master.

Make for the camp of Fionn, here to the west; make thy
couch there, gentle redlipped one, with a man worthy of thee.

With what man should I lie, O great Goll, thou who wert
pleasing to me? Where should I find, west or east, a man equal
to thee?'

With Goll's reply the tragedy deepens, and after further
exchanges he turns to describe his grim plight:

'. . . I am hemmed in by the cliffs; want of food betrays me
and thirst is overcoming me.'

She rejoins with despairing counsels which he angrily
rejects.

With this hasty glance at a subdivision of poetry in syllabic
metres which, though anonymous and unofficial, has sent

ripples into the stream of world literature far and wide, we must turn from the anonymous, untitled poems which in so many cases have survived through mere chance, to the titled and carefully cherished productions of the court poets.

II. *The Court Poet and his Work*

Dá mbáidhtí an dán, a dhaoine,
gan sheanchas, gan sheanlaoidhe,
go bráth acht athair gach fhir
rachaidh cách gan a chluinsin.

Giolla Brighde Mhac Con Midhe, *circa* 1259.

('Were poetry to be suppressed, my friends, with no history,
no ancient lays, save that each had a father, nothing of any
man would be heard hereafter.')

'But such as neither of themselves can sing
Nor yet are sung of others for reward
Die in obscure oblivion . . .'

Edmund Spenser.

Vixere fortes ante Agamemnona
multi; sed omnes illacrimabiles
urgentur ignotique longa
nocte, carent quia vate sacro.

Horace.

('Brave men were living before Agamemnon,
But then they shone not on the poet's page.
And so have been forgotten . . .' Byron).

COURT poetry; praise, elegy, satire; those are the
kinds of verse we are usually thinking of when we
speak of 'bardic poetry', and here the term is not entirely
unjustified, for in some of the earliest documents where the
Celts are mentioned, such poetry is said to be the trade of
the bard: 'They have poets whom they call bards, who sing
songs of eulogy and satire, accompanying themselves on

60

an instrument very like the lyre,' we are told by a Greek writer contemporary with Cicero. And our earliest surviving metrical tracts, which in language date from the Old-Irish period treat primarily of bards and *bairdne*, distinguishing the bard from the *fili*, who studied and taught, and therefore we are told, even the free or noble bards (*soerbaird*) were entitled to an honor-price only half as great as that of the *fili*. The precise nature of the early distinction between bard and *fili*, and the history of the eventual assumption of at least some of the earlier bardic functions by the latter has yet to be fully investigated and cannot be adequately dealt with here. From such evidence as our texts afford, it is at least arguable that the bard made his appearance in Irish society at a relatively late period, that his main functions were eulogy, and satire (including incitement in battle), and that the *fili*, in order to reconcile the Christian church to the survival of his own order in some fashion, arrogated to himself the official use of these bardic functions, allowing his own druidic ones to sink into the background. Be this as it may, what we do know is that throughout the period covered in the court poetry of the classical style that has come down to us, roughly 1200 to 1650, the term bard whenever it appears denotes a subordinate functionary. In a prophecy of evil days to come, preserved in the Book of Leinster and other MSS., one of the expected ills is: 'poets (*filid*) will be childless so that there will be no poets at all, only bards.' (LL 188ᶜ. RC xxvi 45 n.). A 'poet' is *fili, ollamh, ollamh re dán* (master in [poetic] art), *suí re dán* (skilled in [poetic] art), *fear dána, éigeas* (scholar, learned poet). And even in some contemporary English documents (though Spenser, not considering the matter too curiously, knows only 'Bards' for 'Poets') we find the same distinction. For instance, Smyth, the sixteenth-century commentator already cited, though he first gives 'bards' or 'riming septs' (not indeed improperly) as the meaning of *aos dán*, says in the detailed description which follows: 'Now comes the Rymer . . .

61

Also he hathe his Barde, which is a kind of folise fellowe . . .'
(He does not state what the 'Barde's' function is, but see below.) Compare with this Ferghal Mhac an Bhaird's description of his own decayed estate at the close of the sixteenth century: *Mé gan fiú an bhaird do bhuidhin*, 'That I have not even a bard for my retinue.'

The court poet, a *fili*, qualified by a long and rigorous training in language, prosody and various kinds of historical lore (also in some studies less acceptable to the church, spells and charms, etc.) held a commanding place in the social system, a position established by centuries of careful and shrewd use of the gifts and accomplishments of these learned classes. His was an hereditary calling: *mac fileadh agus ua araili* '(to be) the son of a poet and the grandson of another poet' was one of the titles to the highest rank in the profession. He belonged to the aristocracy, to the *nemed*-grades, classes of privileged persons; who, however, could retain their privileges only by strictly observing the obligations entailed by their rank and calling. Thus the poet amongst other obligations had to maintain a high standard in his compositions; to avoid slovenliness or inaccuracy in prosody or in diction. The *cethri srotha déc éicsi* 'the fourteen rivers of poetic inspiration' included *idna láme 7 lánamnais, idna beóil 7 foglomma* 'purity of hand and of wedlock, purity of lips and of learning.'

In the court poetry of the classical period the metrical frame-work of each metre in use is essentially the same as in the earlier lyrical and didactic poems, but for the more ceremonial pieces the rules for the use of ornament are stricter. The number of internal rimes in each stanza and the number and position of alliterating words in each line are precisely determined.

COMPOSING A POEM

Cid dorcha dam im lebaid

'Though I lie in darkness on my couch.'
(Anon. Opening line of a *Dinnshenchus* 'Lore of places' poem).

In the procedure followed in composing a poem we seem
to discern something of the druidic origin of the craft of the
fili. The poet retired to a darkened room or cell, and there,
lying on a couch, he composed his verses unhurriedly. The
practice is described in detail in the Dissertation prefixed to
the Clanricarde Memoirs (Dublin, 1722; the anonymous
author has been identified by Flower, Catalogue of Irish
MSS. in the British Museum III, p. 16, as Thomas
O'Sullevane), and is incidentally alluded to here and there
in the literature, apparently for instance in the line quoted
at the head of this section. An amusing and informing
instance is a late-sixteenth-century poem by Fear Flatha Ó
Gnímh in which he remonstrates humorously with another
poet who has violated etiquette by composing extempore,
in the open air, and on horseback!

Not so did the masters of bygone days, Ó Huiginn,
Ó Dálaigh, Mág Raith, perfect the polished gems of their
art, as for himself:

> Misi féin dá ndearnoinn dán,
> maith leam—lughoide ar seachrán—
> bac ar ghriangha um theachta as-teagh,
> leaptha diamhra gar ndídean.

> Eadrom is eatoil ghlana
> muna n-iadhoinn m'aphradha,
> mar dhlaoi díona ar lés an laoi
> díogha dom ghrés do-ghéntaoi.

'As for myself, should I make a poem, I like—a thing
which keeps me from error—a barrier to keep out the sunlight,
and dim couches to guard me. If I did not close my eyelids

63

between me and the bright rays as a protecting veil against the daylight it would ruin my artistry.' (Quoted from the edition and translation by Bergin, *Studies*, 1920, 2.)

Ag éisdeacht re dréachtaibh 7 re duanlaoidhibh . . . *ga soluisreic i mbéalaibh reacaireadh 7 rioghbhard* 'as they listen to verses and poetic lays (perhaps 'odes') eloquently uttered by declaimers and royal bards' (from a *crosántacht*, i.e. a composition in which a series of *dán díreach* stanzas is interpolated here and there by prose passages, addressed to MacWilliam Burke. The whole has been edited by Father L. McKenna, see *Dioghluim Dána*, p. 379).

'Theyr verses are usually songe at all feasts and meetings, by certayne other persons, whose proper function that is . . .'

Spenser.

The completed poem was recited or chanted to the chief, but not by the poet, for it is here, according to many references both in Irish and English writings, that the function of the bard as the poet's follower is revealed. A common word for the reciter is a borrowed one, *reacaire*, but it is often coupled with *bard* as though the two were synonymous. The bard, however, certainly had charge of the music. The description in the Clanricarde Memoirs is probably reliable: 'The *Action* and *Pronunciation* of the Poem in Presence . . . of the principal Person it related to, was performed with a great deal of Ceremony, in a Consort of Vocal and Instrumental Musick. The Poet himself said nothing, but directed and took care, that every body else did his Part right. The Bards having first had the Composition from him, got it well by heart, and now pronounc'd it orderly, keeping even Pace with a Harp, touch'd upon that Occasion; no other musical Instrument being allow'd of for the said Purpose than this alone.'[1]

[1] Cf. 'Usually the *troubadour* had one or more *joglars* in his service, who performed their master's compositions and might be sent by him to sing a

Another term to denote the declaimer is *marcach duaine*, 'horseman of poetry'. It may originally have been used of one who brought the poem from a distance. There are several references to poems being sent in charge of the reciter to the chief addressed. (See the verses edited by Bergin, beginning *Triall a reacaire, reac m'fhuighle* 'go, my reciter, recite my words,' *Studies*, 1922, 82.)[1]

LANGUAGE

Both in Irish and English writings we find frequent references to the 'learned language' of the poets and their consequent unintelligibility to the vulgar. Stanihurst (who, however, does not seem to have had any practical knowledge of the language either in its vulgar or learned manifestations) is particularly emphatic about this, giving the impression that nobody save the poets themselves could understand the literary dialect. The early rhapsodical style, a kind of rhetorical prose, such as that in the Colloquy of Néde and Ferchertne in their contest for the Poet's Chair is, of course, designedly obscure, abounding in kennings and recondite allusions, but the classical verse is on a different level. Doubtless like any other literary writing it was somewhat over the head of the uncultured listener, though the preservation of so many early modern texts in late paper manuscripts accurately transcribed long after the schools had perished, and the oral transmission of so much Ossianic verse, shows that there was a reasonably large public to

[1] See further Bergin's lecture 'Bardic Poetry' printed in *Journal of the Ivernian Society*, v (1913), 153 f.

---

particular song to the lady in whose honour it had been written.' Chaytor, *The Troubadours of Dante*, p. xv (see p. 21 above). The poems of the *troubadours*, like those of the Irish poets, were sung or chanted to an instrumental accompaniment, see Chaytor *l.c.* pp. xxviii ff., xxxii ff. How far this parallel extends in usage is a matter for investigation. The *troubadour* metres were usually more complicated than the Irish syllabic ones.

appreciate literary compositions. At the dawn of the seventeenth century, Eochu Ó Heódhusa, poet to the Maguires and O'Donnells, humorously declares that he intends to adopt a more popular style:

Le dorchacht na ngrés snoighthe
do bhínnse ag tuilliodh gráine,
ba hí ughachta mhóráin
nár dhíol róghráidh ar ndáinne . . .

Dán bog ar bhél na slighiodh
ós é anois sirthior oraind
cuirfeadsa dhíom na fiacha
go ccead d'iarla Chlann gConaill.

Mo gheallsa ar bhuga ar mhaoile
ni bhérdaois daoithe an bheatha . . .

Beag nach brisiodh mo chroidhe
gach dán roimhe dá gcumainn;
is mór an t-adhbhar sláinte
an nós so táinig chugainn.

'by the obscurity of carven ornament I used to earn disgust; many protested that my verse was unworthy of favour . . ; Free and easy verse on the open road!—since that is what is asked of me I will discharge the debts, by the leave of the Earl of Tyrconnell. The dunces of the world would not beat me in softness and artlessness . . . Every poem I composed hitherto used almost to break my heart; this new fashion that has come to us is a great cause of health.' (From *Ionmholta malairt bhisigh*, edited and translated by Osborn Bergin, *Studies*, 1918, p. 616. The earl is Rury O'Donnell.) But Eochu's innovations here are mainly matters of metre, imperfect rimes and scantness of ornament. His kinsman, Giolla Brighde, makes a graver reference to artificial language in a poem in strict *deibhidhe* prefixed to his *Teagasg Críostaidhe* 'Christian doctrine' (1611):

66

Ag so anois do nimh chugaibh
sreth grianach gheam ccarmugail,
tegaisg thoirtheacha Dé dúin,
troimcheatha do sgé an Sgrioptúir.

Ní thugsam dhóibh, ní díoth soin,
faighreadh a nGaoidhilg grianaigh;
a nDia, a lochthobar na leag,
cia an fothragadh nach fuairsead?

Ní dhernsam, nír dhénta dhamh,
dorcha lé dealradh briathar,
bróin ngemghoirthe niamhtha ó nimh,
briathra dealraighthe an dúilimh.

Lé hóradh bhriathar dá mbeinn,
mór dhíobh fá chiaigh dho chuirfinn,
congmhaid failghe chumhdaigh cloch
urdail na faighne a bhfolach.

'Here for you from heaven is a gleaming row of gorgeous gems, the fruitful teachings of God to us; copious showers cast forth by Scripture. We have not given them, that is no loss, a tempering in lustrous Gaelic; in God, in the lake-spring of jewels, what immersion have they not had? I did not, it was not for me to do, darken with brilliance of words the glistening gem-tempered throng from heaven, the lustrous words of our Creator. Had I busied myself with gilding words, much of them should I have left beneath cloud, the jewelled rings conceal even the the sheath itself.'

The poets did indeed 'write Irish learnedlie' (as Stanihurst puts it); but perhaps not more learnedly than a modern Frenchman writes French. Perhaps not even quite as learnedly, because while they maintained an archaic pronunciation, giving full value to the old lenited forms of intervocalic consonants which had long disappeared from common speech, they did not always reject innovations in grammar; for instance, *atá mé* may be substituted for *atú* (*metri gratia*). However, this blend of archaism and dialectal eclecticism proved in prose also an efficient instrument for

67

clear and logical expression, and the feeling for style found in the best of the early nineteenth-century writers derives from it.

STYLE

> Goirthear Teach Tuathail d'Éirinn,
> Cró Chuinn is Fonn finnFhéilim.
> Iath Iúghoine is Achadh Airt
> Críoch Cobhthaigh is Clár Chormaic.

('Ireland is called the House of Tuathal, the Fold of Conn, and Land of fair Felim, Meadow of Iughoine and Field of Art, Territory of Cobhthach and Plain of Cormac.'

Aodh Ó Domhnaill in *Iomarbháigh na bhfileadh*.)

To appreciate the court poetry fully, one must be acquainted with the mythico-historical background against which the poet weaves his theme. Just as much of such a poem as Milton's *Lycidas* is unintelligible to those ignorant of the historical reasons which caused this strange medley of shepherds, fauns, saints and archangels to appear in the poem, so Tadhg Óg Ó Huiginn's references to native eponymous deities, Grecians, Spaniards, pagan and Christian kings, though more consistently related to a general scheme than Milton's figures, can only bewilder an unprepared audience. Perhaps I may be permitted here to quote from the Introduction to the Irish Texts Society edition of the poems of Tadhg Dall Ó Huiginn, p. xlix:

'The machinery . . . of historical allusion . . . has for a basis the official history as represented in *Lebar Gabála* (The Book of Invasions) and the received genealogies from the earliest occupations down to the death of Maol Seachluinn, who is implicitly referred to as the last high-king of Ireland . . . When the exigencies of the case require it, the poets are ready to admit or suggest that the Milesian claims have been superseded, as when Torna Ó Maoil Chonaire . . . adds to the six occupations enumerated in *Lebar Gabála* a seventh, that of the Fitzgeralds'.

68

The figurative language, kennings and metaphors, frequently depend upon this tradition; the poetic names for Ireland: *Inis Fáil, Teach Tuathail, Fonn Feradhaigh*, etc., etc., each reflects some item of ancient historic or mythological lore known and cherished by contemporary listeners. There are many other poetical epithets for Ireland: *Fiadh Fuinidh* 'land of the west'; *Clár (magh, tulach*, etc.) *na bhFionn* 'Plain (hill, etc.) of the Fair ones'; *Banbha, Fódla* are, of course, common. The name of a part may be used to denote the whole, very common in this use is *Teamhair* 'Tara', and any of its ancient bynames, viz. *Cathair Chrooinn, Druim Caoin, Liathdruim, Tulach an Trír*, and others. The most frequent of all these 'kennings' is *Breagha* 'Bregia', the Leinster territory so conspicuously associated with the rulers of Ireland both in ancient and more modern times, the territory wherein Tara stood and where the great pre-historic monuments of Dowth and Newgrange are still to be seen, as well as *Bóinn* 'the Boyne'. This name is always in the genitive (*Breagha* is pl. of *brí* 'hill'), depending on some word such as *rí, flaith, laoch*, etc. ('king, prince, hero, of'), or *fir, sluagh, foireann* ('men, host, of') or other word denoting population, or *Magh, Clár* 'plain', etc.

The complimentary epithets of persons are of various kinds, referring to nobility of birth, beauty of form, strength, prowess, hospitality, success in war or in love. Often they are metonymical: *súil mhall* 'steady (or stately) glance'; *lámh thréan* 'strong arm'; *gruadh ghlan* 'bright cheek'; *folt tiugh, ciabh chas* 'thick or wavy hair,' etc. etc. The meta-phorical epithets show a widely extended range: animals known or unknown, real or fabulous, e.g.: *coileán, damh, leómhan, beithir, gríobh* ('whelp, ox, lion, bear, griffin'); birds and fishes, *seabhac* ('hawk,' denoting keeness in battle), *eala, géis* ('swan', for grace and beauty), *eó, éigne, maighre* ('salmon, trout', probably implying wisdom, referring to the inspiration derived from the *cna Seghsa* 'nuts of Seghais,' which dropped into the Boyne or Shannon to be eaten by the salmon, according to the legend). Plant names, etc., *géag, craobh, cnú* ('branch, nut'), *crann fíneamhna* 'vine-stalk'; *subh, or sugh fíneamhna* 'fruit or juice of the vine,' *bile* 'ancient tree'. Natural phenomena are used freely: *grían, éasga, réalta* ('sun, moon, star'), etc., *grinneal áigeóin gan forus* 'unfathomable ocean bed' (Tadhg Dall of Mac William Burke). It seems very likely that the use of some of these words in this way came in with the Christian Latin poetry and derive ultimately from the Bible. Compare the Old-Irish litanies, and see p. liv of the Introduction to Tadhg Dall, already cited.

Each of these metaphorical words is in most cases followed by a dependent genitive, a place- or population-name, e.g., *leómhan Éirne* 'lion of the Erne' (O'Donnell, Maguire); *géis grianDoire* 'swan of bright Derry' (Maguire); *dreagan Teamhrach* 'dragon of Tara' (id.); *an coillbhile ós chlár Uladh* 'the ancient hazel-tree of Ulster's plain' (Turloch Luineach). Congruity is not always obvious in these references; Turlogh is in the same poem styled *cleith béildearg Bhóroimhe* 'red-lipped hero (*lit.* shaft) of Bóroimhe,' i.e. of the place in Thomond whence Brian Bóroimhe 'Brian Boru' was so called. MacWilliam Burke is described as *sdéad mearghroighe ó mhúr Eamhna* 'steed from the swift mares of Eamhain's rampart.'

A detailed account of the complimentary style would run to many pages, and cannot be attempted here. I shall conclude this brief sketch by quoting a few illustrative stanzas:

Tadhg Dall, of Eoghan Óg Mhac Suibhne:

> Maighre séanta a sruth Fhinne,
> lá gréine i ndiaidh dílinne;
> gnúis mhórdha is céimleasg i gcath,
> éinfhleasg órdha na nUltach.

'Precious salmon from the stream of the Finn, a sunny day after a downpour; stately figure, cool (*lit.* uneager of pace) in conflict, the Ulstermen's gilded stem.'

Another Mac Suibhne, Maol Mórdha is thus recalled:

> Ár luibh íce, ár n-ortha chodail,
> ár gcraobh thoraidh, ár dteach séad;
> mír cruadha nár éimdhidh aoinfhear,
> éinghein bhuadha Gaoidheal nGréag.

'Our healing herb, our sleep charm, our fruitful branch, our house of treasure; a piece of steel (yet) one who never denied any man, most precious offspring of the Grecian Gaels.'

POEMS OF PRAISE, PROTEST, ETC.

The earliest specimen of encomium in *dán díreach* that has come down to us is in the St. Paul Codex, a manuscript ascribed by some scholars to the eighth century, by others to the ninth.[1] The metre is *rannaigheacht bheag* with internal rime and consonance but the arrangement of the internal rimes is not so strict as in the later panegyrics, and in most of the eight stanzas, *aicill* (rime between the end-word of a line with one in the interior of the following) is substituted for consonance, e.g.:

> Mac Diarmata dil damsa
> cid iarfacta ni insa,
> a molad maissiu maenib
> luaidfider laedib limmsa.

'Son of Diarmait dear to me, though it be to be asked it is not difficult, his praise is comelier than treasures, it will be sung in lays by me.'

One of the earliest complete poems in the strict classical style that have survived, perhaps the earliest, is that addressed to Raghnall, 'ua' of Gofraidh an Mhearáin, or Gofraidh Mearánach, king of Dublin and the Isles.[2] As Gofraidh died, according to the Annals of Ulster, in 1095, his grandson would normally have flourished in the mid-twelfth century. It is possible, however, since Raghnall has

[1] See *Thesaurus Palaeohibernicus*, Stokes and Strachan, ii, p. 295.
[2] Edited and translated with notes by Brian Ó Cuív, *Éigse*, vii.

not been[1] identified, that 'ua' is here to be rendered not 'grandson' but descendant, which would allow a later dating. There is no apparent reason, however, to suppose the poem to be later than the first half of the thirteenth century. The metre is the same as that of the St. Paul poem just quoted, but unlike that, most strict and elaborate, with rime, consonance and alliteration perfect in every stanza. It is also remarkable for the mythological references. Here are a few stanzas:

> Eamhain abhlach na n-iobhar
> sleamhain barrdhath a bileadh;
> baile nua fan dubh droighean
> inar hoileadh Lugh ua an fhileadh.

> Eamhain na n-abhall gcumhra,
> Teamhair Mhanann gan mheabhla;
> as iad cuaine saor Sadhbha
> abhla craobh n-uaine nEamhna.

> Tusa mac Sadhbha saoire,
> as tú an tslat abhla as áille;
> cá dia do bhrú na Bóinne
> do-róine ria tú i dtáidhe?

> A Raghnuill, a rí an diongna,
> radhruim Dá Thí ar tí th'earla;
> do-ghéabhae, a mheic shaoir Shadbha,
> labhra ón leic i dtaoibh Teamhra.

> Dámadh leat slóigh fhear bhfuinidh,
> ó Bhóinn go mbean re Tibhir,
> mó dheit ar mhil 's ar mheadhair
> Eamhain mheic Lir mheic Mhidhir.

'Apple-treed Eamhain of the yews! Her tree-tops of polished colour; bright stead where the blackthorn flourishes, where Lugh the poet's grandson was reared. Eamhain of the fragrant

---

[1] Dr. Ó Cuív has now shown (*l.c.* p. 283 f.) that he was great-grandson of Gofraidh, and became King of Man in 1187.

apple-trees, Tara of Man untreacherous; the noble brood of Sadhbh are the fruit of the green branches of Eamhain. Thou art the son of noble Sadhbh; thou art the loveliest apple-branch. What god from the Boyne begot thee from her by stealth? O Raghnall, king of the stronghold, the great Ridge of Dá Thí [i.e. Ireland] seeks thy tresses; thou, O noble son of Sadhbh, wilt get an utterance from the flagstone beside Tara. Hadst thou the hosts of the men of the west, from Boyne till it touches the Tiber,[1] more to thee for honey and mirthful feasting were Eamhain of the son of Ler son of Midhir' (§§5–9).

In cold translation, lacking the gorgeous metrical robe of the original, this is too quaint in expression to impress as poetry to-day. Here Eamhain Abhlach, the Avalon of Arthurian romance, is placed in the Isle of Man, the isle associated in legend with Manannán. The stark reference in the third stanza above recalls the great pagan cemetery in the Boyne valley, celebrated in a poem by Cionaoth Ua Hartagán as the burial-place of many of the pre-Christian kings of Ireland, but also associated with a past even more shadowy, with Lugh, Aí mac Ollaman, Carbre son of Etan, and the Dagda; mythic figures connected in legend with poetic inspiration.

Although the compliments and methods of reference in the panegyrics or odes are usually (not invariably) stereotyped, the poems themselves do not follow an unchanging pattern of composition. There are certain requisites, of course, for encomium: the person addressed must be fully identified; the names of his father and grandfather must be given, and his general descent made clear. Often the mother's name and lineage are also recorded. It has to be shown whether he is head of the clan, as Ó Néill, Mág Uidhir, or merely a *damhna*, 'Mac Í Néill, Mac Méig Uidhir.' The

---

[1] According to the *Dindshenchus* the Boyne was a far-flowing river, reappearing in Britain as the Severn, in Rome as the Tiber, in the east as Jordan, etc., etc. (*Metrical Dindshenchus*, ed. Gwynn, iii, 28).

opening line is usually some striking expression, an aphorism or proverb: *Fulang annróidh adhbhar sóidh* 'Endurance of hardship is a source of pleasure'; *Mairg do-ní deimhin dá dhóigh* 'Woe to him who makes a certainty of his hope'; or it may be a personal reference or appeal; *Bíodh aire ag Ultaibh ar Aodh* 'Let the Ulstermen take heed of Aodh'; *Beir eólas dúinn a Dhomhnaill* 'Be our guide, O Domhnall'; sometimes with vaguer reference, *Menic fríoth Éire a hEamhain* 'Often hath Erin been won from (i.e. by a chief in) Eamhain.' This initial line sets the theme which is unfolded in the succeeding verses. In the inaugural odes and in poems of remonstrance or appeal, the argument is in most cases clinched by an apologue, drawn from the store of *scéla* and *foscéla* prescribed as part of the curriculum of the poetic schools. The example may be from native legend or from foreign sources; Cú Chulainn or Conaire, Hector or Caesar may be recalled: the *Legenda aurea* and other collections of European mediaeval lore are frequently utilized. The poem concludes with renewed compliments and promises. In many cases some verses of compliment to the chief's lady are added after the ending proper, these additional lines are 'closed' in the same way as the main poem, by ending with the same word or syllable with which the latter began. Some poets regularly conclude with a stanza addressed to the patron saint.

O'Donovan saw in the work of the court poets the analogue of the modern newspaper (see O'Grady's Catalogue, p. 340), and it is certainly comparable in some measure with that of the prose pamphleteers of the seventeenth and eighteenth centuries. Such unsympathetic observers as Spenser and Smyth saw nothing in the composition of the Irish poets, despite their 'savour of sweete witt and good invention' and the sprinkling of 'prety flowers of theyr owne naturall devise, which gave good grace and comliness unto them,' save incitements to war and other mischievous activities. These views, however, though not entirely without excuse, do not take in the whole scene. Calls to battle there certainly are, but perhaps even more common is the shrewd and tactfully phrased eirenicon adducing cogent arguments in favour of peaceful and cautious conduct. We also find personal complaints against the patron (without resort to satire), poems of remonstrance; expostulations uttered as it were more in surprise and sorrow than in anger; appeals for redress of some injustice, for reparation for injury inflicted by the chief himself or by his family or followers. On the other hand, we find the poet pleading for forgiveness and restoration to favour after some slight which he has inadvertently, perhaps *in vino*, inflicted on his patron. The general tone of such pieces is as a rule strikingly independent, but the skilful blending of admonition and flattery, appeal and threat, exhibits all the resources of this poetic style.

While the work of the court poets is in form strictly traditional and conservative, it is at the same time contemporary. Throughout its period it is, apart from homiletic and theological writing, the only contemporary literature of an appreciable amount that has survived, and it is undoubtedly a literature of the privileged classes. It was also a literature based on conventions; a linguistic convention whereby it was composed in a literary dialect based on historical correctness combined with a wide degree of liberty in the use of local innovations; and a political convention based on an ingenious compromise between contemporary fact and historic claims; between what had been and what was. Thus all over Ireland we find leading chieftains hailed in inaugural panegyrics as prospective high kings, heirs or successors of Tuathal or Niall or Brian, etc. When the candidate is of the more recently established foreign blood, his claim (never, of course, more seriously intended than that of the others) is easily justified; for instance of Richard de Burgo (Riocard a Búrc) a fifteenth-century poet, Maol Seachluinn Ó Huiginn, proclaims:

> Cairt chloidhimh—cá cairt is fearr?
> cairt Riocaird ar Ráth Raoileann.

'The charter of the sword—what better one is there?—
is Richard's charter to Ráth Raoileann (i.e., Ireland).'

And he continues:

> Ós cairt chloidhimh chosnus sin,
> ionann ceart chloinne Mílidh
> is na mBúrcfhear dar ghiall goil
> ar fiadh gcúirtgheal ó gCobhthaigh.

'Since the charter he contends by is of the sword, then the
claim of the children of Míl is equal to that of the Burkes
to the bright-castled land of Cobhthach's line.'

The same argument is used with more detail by Tadhg
Dall a century later (to the disgust of Charles O'Conor of
Belanagare).

Tuathal Ó Huiginn, another fifteenth-century poet,
uses the argument in quizzical fashion in a poem urging
Eoghan Ó Raghallaigh to ignore any grant by English
charter: Greece, he reminds the young man, is the native
land of the Gaels; thence they travelled to Ireland, sojourn-
ing in Spain on the way; not a man of them is in his hereditary patrimony; the sword, charter for which no seal was
required, is the only one Eoghan needs or on which he can
rely. Gofraidh Fionn Ó Dálaigh, regarded by the poets
themselves as the most gifted and accomplished of them all,
a reputation amply justified by his surviving poems, sums
up the matter frankly in some cynical lines addressed to the
Earl of Desmond:

> Flaitheas nach gabhaid Gaoidhil
> geallmaoid dóibh i nduanlaoidhibh;
> a ráthughadh dhúibh níor dhluigh,
> gnáthughadh dhúinn a dhéanamh.

'A sovranty they never get we promise to the Gaels in our
odes; you need not take any notice of this, it is our custom.'

But not only the Gaels are thus cozened:

> Dá chineadh dá gcumthar dán
> i gcrích Éireann na n-uarán,
> na Gaoidhilse ag boing re bladh,
> is Goill bhraoininnse Breatan.

> I ndán na nGall gealltar linn
> Gaoidhil d'ionnarba a hÉirinn;
> Goill do shraoineadh tar sáil sair
> i ndán na nGaoidheal gealltair.

'There are two kindreds for whom poetry is composed in Ireland of the cool springs—the Gaels, known to fame, and the English of Britain's dewy isle. In poetry for the English we promise that the Gael shall be banished from Ireland; in poetry for the Gaels we promise that the English shall be routed across the sea.'

To frown deeply at such sentiments would perhaps be to miss the perspective of history. The main patrons of Gofraidh Fionn and Ó Huiginn were respectively the de Burgos and the Fitzgeralds, powerful Anglo-Norman families who were satisfied to reign in Ireland as Irish chieftains. These poets of the fourteenth-fifteenth centuries could risk a little playfulness. Things were sterner in the late Tudor period. In a poem addressed to Turloch Luineach, Tadhg Dall recalls that chieftain's dissatisfaction with vagueness in the panegyrics presented to him at a special entertainment. O'Grady understood the lack complained of to be a precise statement of Turloch's right to the title 'Ó Néill'; 'something special to back him against his able and indefatigable competitor, the Baron of Dungannon' (afterwards Earl of Tyrone), see *Brit. Mus. Catalogue of Ir. Manuscripts*, I, 434.

SATIRE

'Greedie of praise they be, & fearfull of dishonour, and to this end they esteeme their poets who write Irish learnedlie and pen their sonets heroicall, for the which they are bountifullie rewarded, if not they send out libels in dispraise, thereof the lords and gentlemen stand in great awe.'

Richard Stanihurst.

Courts have proverbially a corrosive effect on morality and political integrity, and the very term 'court poet' carries with it a disquieting suggestion of insincerity, sycophancy and fear of disfavour. But the Irish poet-courtier had an advantage lacking to palace favourites in other lands; if he feared the displeasure of his lord, the latter might fear his even more. The wound from satire or lampoon was not only sore and rankling to the over-sensitive pride of an Irish nobleman, but, according to popular belief, it might even prove mortal. The expression 'loss of face', which in recent years has entered into European political commentaries as a loan from China, was in constant use in ancient Ireland with the same meaning: *meth n-enech* (*lit.* 'loss of face') expresses 'dishonour', 'loss of status through conduct unfitting to it'. For a prince or nobleman, niggardliness, refusal of hospitality, rejection of an appeal for a gift (especially, of course, any solicitation by a poet) was the surest and most deadly way to damage one's reputation.

I do not propose to deal at length with the subject of satire. It is one which leads far into folklore and magic, matters not indeed alien to literary history in general, or to the history of Irish poetry in particular, but lying beyond the scope of this short survey. Naturally, not many complete satires have been preserved. A few scurrilous quatrains or passages occur here and there, usually in illustration of some metrical or linguistic usage, and consisting, when the words are at all interpretable, mainly of rows of disparaging epithets. But there are also more subtly expressed examples.

In a concise little Middle-Irish tract on the subject preserved in the Book of Ballymote, satire is said to be of three kinds, viz. *aisnéis*, defined as 'insulting speech, without harmony' (i.e., not in rimed verse), an example is cited: a

78

satirist was dissatisfied with the food given to him in the house of a certain nobleman. 'Shall salt be sprinkled on your food?' said the servant. No, said he, for there is nothing to sprinkle it on, unless it be sprinkled on my tongue, and that isn't necessary; it is bitter enough already.' *Ail* 'reproach' is 'an opprobrious epithet which sticks'. The third kind, *aircetal aíre*, is subdivided into ten species, the nature and exemplification of which involve more explanation and annotation than it would be profitable to attempt here. The first in the list, *mac bronn*, is discussed in an article by Professor David Greene (*Éigse*, v, 230 ff.) which includes a poem transliterated and translated from the Dean of Lismore's Book. From this poem it appears that the term means a satire *in posse*, as it were; ready, but so far unuttered. The eighth in the list, *lánaer* 'full satire' is one in which the victim is clearly identified. The last, *glám dícend*, appears to have been a particularly deadly kind, involving an elaborate ritual, of which the description is quoted below from another tract.

The use and effect of satire is illustrated in various ancient legends, notably in the story of Caiér, king of Connacht, who was satirized by his nephew, the poet Néde, unjustly, the occasion having been arranged at the instigation of Caiér's wife, who plotted to set Néde in her husband's place. Since no king with a blemish could retain his throne, she aimed to cause one: 'Make a satire for him that he may have a blemish. The man with a blemish shall not reign.' 'That is not an easy thing for me to do. The man will not refuse me. There is nothing in the world in his possession that he will not give me.' 'I know something he will not give thee, that is, the knife that was brought to him from Albu; he will not give thee that. It is a forbidden thing for him that it should be taken from him.'

Néde entreated Caiér to give him the knife. 'Woe, woe!' replied Caiér, 'It is *geis*[1] for me to part with it.' Néde then

---

[1] *i.e.* 'prohibited thing,' 'taboo'.

composed for him a satire of the kind called *glám dícend*, so that three blisters appeared on his face. The language of the satire is obscure and most of the words in the quatrain of which it consists are glossed in the manuscript, but not very helpfully for the modern reader. The hapless king passed his hands over his face and finding the blemishes which betrayed his plight, fled for refuge to Dún Cermna. The poet took the kingship, and after a year's reign was one day seized with remorse for having afflicted Caiér. He then journeyed to Dún Cermna in Caiér's chariot with Caiér's wife by his side. Caiér's host describes to him the approaching visitor; from his response, his true rank, which had not hitherto been known in his refuge, was recognized. 'This is the speech of a king,' said his host. 'Ah no, my soul!' said Caiér. With that he went out of the house and hid himself in a cleft behind the *dún*. There Néde's dogs tracked him and on seeing Néde he died from shame. At Caiér's death the rock exploded and a splinter from it struck the guilty poet in the eye.

Of the method of applying the *glám dícend* we have a curious account in one of the early metrical tracts:

There is fasting on the land of the king for whom the (unrequited) poem has been composed and counsel is taken with thirty warriors (or perhaps the literal 'laymen' is meant here) and thirty bishops and thirty poets about making a satire afterwards. And it is unlawful for them to hinder the satire once the reward has been refused. It only remains for the poet accompanied by six who have respectively the six degrees of poetry to go before sunrise to a mound where seven territories meet, and the chief poet faces the land of the king he is about to revile and they all have their backs to a thorn which stands on the summit of the hill, and there is a north wind, and each man carries in his hand a stone and a spike from the thorn and speaks into both of them a stanza in the measure called *laídh*. The chief poet says his stanza first, and then the other poets chant theirs in unison, and each puts his stone and his spike at the base of the thorn, and if it is they that are in fault the ground of the hill swallows them up; if it is the king, however, that is in fault the ground swallows him and his wife and his child and his horse and his weapons and his clothing and his hound.[1]

The satirical verses of the notorious Aonghus na n-aor 'A. of the satires' (see O'Grady's *Brit. Mus. Catalogue*, 443 ff.; the elegy there discussed has been edited by Father Lambert McKenna, *Dioghluim Dána*, p. 223 ff.) in detraction of the ruling families of Ireland are mainly descriptive of the sad lack of hospitality which he alleges that he found everywhere as he journeyed throughout the country. A few samples of this unattractive, and indeed very dull composition will suffice to illustrate the style:

> Gabhar truagh i dtigh Í Bhroin
> 's gan luadh ar dhigh 'na dheaghaidh.

'In the house of Ó B. a lean goat, and no talk of a drink to follow.'

In another mansion:

> A chuil bheag úd ar bhun na gaibhle,
>   dá mb'eól duit déanamh fuadach,
> bhéarfá mo chuid aráin 's ime
>   cois na Finne leat go suarach.

'Little fly on the edge of the gable, if thou didst know how to steal thou wouldst carry off with thee easily my share of bread and butter beside the Finn.'

More personal abuse also occurs in Aonghus's satire:

> Ní aoraimse acht mná maithe,
> clanna ríogh nó rofhlaithe;
> atá sise saor mar soin,
> níor aor mise bhur máthair.

'None but gentlewomen do I satirize, the children of kings or great noblemen; so she is exempt; I never satirized your mother.'

[1] See *Irische Texte*, iii, pp. 96–97.

Scorn is incisively expressed in:

> Ní raibh luadh i nÉirinn air,
> 's ní raibh iomrádh i nAlbain;
> do-rine mé leas Uí Fhlainn,
> nírbh fheas é muna n-aorfainn.

'He was not talked about in Ireland, he was not discussed in Scotland; I have been of advantage to O F., he would not have been known if I had not satirized him.'

PERSONAL POEMS

Not all that the court poet composed was official. He used his art for personal objects as well. Much of the later love poetry treated of above, pp. 45, 53, is the work of court poets. As well as official elegies we have such pieces as Gofraidh Fionn's lament for his son Eóghan, in which he apostrophizes the cross which calls him to memory:

> Is tú, a chros an mheic mhuirnigh,
> thug mé anocht go neamhshuilbhir;
> a dhlúthchros fá dtú ag tuirse,
> tú mhúchfas mo mheadhairse . . .
>
> Atá an chros ler cráidheadh mé
> ar deilbh do chroise, a Choimdhe;
> ar a los go dtí dod thigh
> an tí dan cros an chrossin.
>
> Bheith ar chúl chroise Eóghain
> dom athtuirse oisgeólaidh;
> díon ar slógh é agus gidh eadh,
> ar brón, a Dhé, ní dídean.

He recalls tales of other fathers; Cathbhaidh the Druid, who died from grief for his son Geanann:

> Cathbhaidh mar do-chuaidh reamhainn
> d'éag do chumhaidh chaoimhGheanainn,
> mó a fhachain, gá dás gan dol
> an t-athair ór fhás Eóghan?

And the Daghdha, who roamed the world carrying his sick son, Cearmaid, on his back till he found his cure:

> Mo mhacsa ó nach mé an Daghdha
> súil le a éirghe is éadtarbha;
> ní faghair dar mbuain a broid
> an bhuaidh do chabhair Cearmoid.

He concludes:

> Ní fhuilnginn an uair do mhar
> do mhéad ár n-annsa d'Eóghan—
> choidhche gé do-near anois—
> an fear dá oidhche im' éagmhais.

> Mar tú dá bhás ní bhiadh mé
> dámadh neach eile a oide,
> cúis asar fhoide, a Dhé, a dhol—
> is mé dob oide d'Eóghan.

> An tEóghansa is éigin dún
> déanamh seach an bhfionn bhfoltúr;
> tairnig a sheal, gá dám dhó?
> gidh eadh, gá dál is deacro?

'It is thou, O cross of the merry lad, that hast made me cheerless this night; O firm cross by which I sorrow, 'tis thou shalt quench my happiness . . . The cross that hath grieved me is shaped like thine, O Lord; because of it may he whose cross it is come to Thy house. To shelter by Eóghan's cross will release my sorrow again, a protection from an army is it, and yet, O God, it is no protection from grief . . . Cathbhaidh before my time died of regret for fair Geanann; since the cause is greater why has not also died the father from whom Eóghan sprang? . . . My son, since I am not the Daghdha, it is profitless to expect him to arise; there is not got to snatch me from sorrow the magic that helped Cearmoid . . . Whilst he lived, such was my affection for Eóghan, I could not endure his absence from me for two nights, though now I endure it for always. I should not be as I am from his death had some one else been his teacher, a cause from which his passing is the more wearying—'tis I was Eóghan's teacher.

This Eóghan, we must now renounce the fair bright-haired fellow; his time has finished, why continue?—yet what fate is harder?' (§§ 2, 13, 14, 26, 37–39. The poem is edited in full by Father McKenna, *Dioghluim Dána*, p. 196 ff.).

Another moving piece is Tadhg Óg Ó Huiginn's lament for his brother and teacher, Fearghal Ruadh; it is edited and translated by Bergin, *Studies* 1924, 85 ff.

The last elegy from which I shall quote here is of the thirteenth century, Muireadhach Albanach's lament for his dead wife, a poem wherein all the artistry of the craft is skilfully and effectively applied. The unique copy in the Book of the Dean of Lismore is transliterated, edited and translated by Bergin, *Studies* 1924.

> M'anam do sgar riomsa a-raoir,
>   calann ghlan dob ionnsa i n-uaigh;
> rugadh bruinne maordha mín
>   is aonbhla lín uime uainn . . .
>
> Mo chéadghrádh a dearc mhall mhór,
>   déadbhán agus cam a cliabh;
> nochar bhean a colann chaomh
>   ná a taobh re fear romham riamh.
>
> Fiche bliadhna inne ar-aon,
>   fá binne gach bliadhna ar nglór,
> go rug éinleanabh déag dhún,
>   an ghéag úr mhéirleabhar mhór.

'My soul parted from me last night; a pure body that was dear is in the grave; a gentle stately bosom has been taken from me with one linen shroud about it . . . Her large gentle eye was my first love, her bosom was curved and white as ivory; her fair body belonged to no man before me. Twenty years we spent together; sweeter was our converse every year; she bore me eleven children, the tall fresh lithe-fingered branch.' (§§1, 10, 11).

THE RELIGIOUS VERSE OF THE COURT POETS

Though as categories, as already mentioned, poet and churchman remained distinct, not only did many court poets eventually pass into church orders, but some who remained laymen devoted their most elaborate work to religious themes. We have a great mass of this later religious verse in the strict style. Much, perhaps most of it, fails to convey the impression of spontaneity and religious simplicity found in the earlier, less elaborated religious verse, still there is much that shows real fervour and sincerity. There are poems in praise of the Saviour and the Blessed Virgin; of the saints and archangels. These are usually in the same encomiastic style as the secular poems. It has been already remarked that the metaphors and figures used in the court poetry were evidently in many instances traceable to Christian-Latin origins, verse or prose, so in turn these epithets appear again in the later religious eulogies. Another kind is the homiletic, poems on the vanity of worldly ambition; the joys in store for the earnest Christian; the terrors of Doomsday and the need for early repentance. Some of these are undoubtedly renderings of Latin originals, for instance there is preserved in the Book of O'Conor Don an anonymous verse rendering of St. Bernard's *Formula honestae vitae*.

Very common themes are naturally the Crucifixion, the Five Wounds; the Piercing Lance. The treatment of these themes is in most cases formal, stylistic. The poet loves to play with, if I may so put it, the *impossibile* of the Faith; the Trinity and the Virgin birth. The symbolism of later Marian poetry provided much that appealed to the Irish taste for paradox. These matters are discussed authoritatively by Father Lambert McKenna in his Introduction to his religious anthology *Dán Dé* and also in his edition of the poems of Pilib Bocht Ó Huiginn.

To judge by their frequency in manuscripts the most widely

85

appreciated religious poems were those attributed to the thirteenth-century poet Donnchadh Mór Ó Dálaigh. These include (although Father McKenna thinks the attribution is uncertain) two very interesting ones on the Cross, in which the mediaeval legends of its origin from the Tree of Paradise are used, as well as other symbolistic explanations. These are really fine poems in their way, not unfit to be compared in some measure with some of the well-known Latin pieces on the same theme. I quote the opening verses of one:

Sbéacláir na cruinne an chroch naomh,
crann suaithnidh na sleas ndonnchaomh;
séala an chroinnse na gcóig gcneadh
róid is soillse re silleadh.

Croch Íosa, mionn cabhra cáigh,
mór ngné asa ngairthear sbéacláir
don órchuanna thiormghlain tais
d' fhiodhbhaidh phórchuanna Pharthais . . .

Dá taobh táinig an tsoillse
do sgaoil doirche an domhuinse;
ní sbéacláir ar nach cáir cion,
do bháidh céadcháir an Choimdheadh.

'A beacon to the world is the holy Cross, conspicuous tree of fair brown surfaces; roads that are the brightest to look on are the seals of this tree of the five wounds. The cross of Jesus, relic which gives succour to all; many are the kinds in which the golden-comely bright dry supple one from the fair seed of the wood of paradise is called a beacon . . . From its side came the light that dispersed the darkness of this world; it is not a beacon unworthy of trust, that which drowned (*i.e.* expunged) the Lord's original claim (*i.e.* freed repentant man from the consequence of the Fall).'

Donnchadh Mór is known only as a religious poet; his kinsman, the proud and hot-tempered Muireadhach Albanach, who considered the slaying of a minor official an inadequate reason for his own banishment, addressed poems to the

O'Donnells and the Burkes, but he also composed some religious pieces, see Father L. McKenna's *Aithdioghluim Dána*, i, p. xxxiii. The poem on the Cross *Marthain duit, a chroch an Choimdheadh* (one of those mentioned above) is attributed to him in the Dean of Lismore's Book, though elsewhere it is given to Donnchadh Mór. Gofraidh Fionn has left several religious poems, including *Mairg mheallas muirn an tsaoghail*, a very fine specimen of this poet's easy, graceful style:

> Flaitheamhnas mór ar mhuirn mbig,
> beatha shíor ar sheal ngairid;
> tréigean Dé is diombuaidh an dáil
> ar ré ndiombuain an domhnáin.
>
> Sódh na sochraide neamhdha
> atá thuas mun dTighearna,
> gach sódh fa nimh seacha soin
> is beatha fhir i n-uamhaidh.
>
> A dhaoine dá ndáiltear rath
> leis nach beag méad a meadhrach;
> bhar sódh is uime is lór libh
> gan sódh is uille d'fhaicsin.

'To barter a great kingdom for sorry cheer, life everlasting in exchange for a short season, to abandon God for the sake of a fleeting term in this miserable world is a transaction without profit. The joy of the heavenly hosts around the Lord above—compared with that every joy neath heaven is the life of one in a cave. O ye to whom fortune is apportioned, and deem its pleasure sufficient, the reason your joys (here) suffice you is that you have seen no greater.'

The apologue of the child born in prison follows. The whole poem is in Father McKenna's *Dioghluim Dána*, pp. 109 ff.

To give a complete idea of a religious poem of the more serious kind, it would have to be given in full and this is not feasible here. Unfortunately, most of the later religious poems suffer from a literary defect very common in the classical poetry; they are too long. The content may be quite small, the vessel imposingly large. A select anthology of the best religious poems is a desideratum. Such an anthology should include an investigation into Latin sources, a work which has not yet been seriously attempted. Now that Father McKenna's labours have provided a large corpus of the Irish texts, a beginning could be made.

THE 'CONTENTION OF THE BARDS'

Even such a brief account as this of Irish court poetry would be incomplete without at least some mention of the 'Contention of the Bards', as it is usually called in English, more correctly *Iomarbháigh na bhfileadh* 'Contention (lit. contention, or more accurately 'counter-boasting') of the Poets,' a production of the early years of the seventeenth century. Verse-contests of various kinds are common enough in Irish literature, early and late; this one is entitled in some manuscripts *Iomarbháigh Leithe Mogha 7 Leithe Cuinn* 'Contest between Leath Mhogha (the Southern Half) and Leath Chuinn (the Northern Half)', that is between the families descended from Éber son of Míl and those descended from Eremón son of Míl. The original challenge is thrown down in a poem feigned to be the work of Torna Éigeas, foster-father of Niall of the Nine Hostages. In this it is asserted that Corc of Cashel (standing for southern claims) submitted to Niall as his overlord. The challenge is taken up by a Clare poet, Tadhg Mac Dáire Mac Bruaideadha, who is answered by a Leath Chuinn poet, Lughaidh Ó Cléirigh, and several others join in. All the traditional learning of the poetic order is brought into play, legendary history, genealogy, ancient poetic rhapsodies, etymology, etc. Much of the argument seems frankly humorous. One of Lughaidh's in favour of the Northern Half is that during the time it was supreme two score lakes and rivers burst forth; no such benefits occurred under southern supremacy, to which Tadhg, having first remarked that if the works of the Creator in any place are to be put to the credit of its mundane rulers, the birth of Our Lord in Bethlehem could be attributed to Herod, he goes on:

> Gach loch, gach linn dá labhra,
> ós dóibh féin téid i dtarbha,
> fuil Éibhir is dóibh do ling,
> ar a gcuid féin don Éirinn.

> Atáid a lán do lochaibh
> is araile do shrothaibh
> agar mhó d'inis Banbha
> a ndíoth iná ndeaghtharbha.

> Báidhtear leó, ní sochar saor,
> ceathra agus daoine maraon;
> gan f héar gan ioth congbhaid soin
> a mbí fútha don talmhain.

> Gibé maith nó saith do-niad,
> nocha maoidhte ar éinrígh iad,
> acht ar an Rígh is rí ar nimh,
> nár iarr congnamh fá ndéinimh.

'Every lake or water you mention, since it is a profit to them in their own part of Ireland, it is for Eber's line it sprang forth. There are many lakes, and some rivers too, that are a loss rather than a profit to Banbha's isle. Both cattle and people are drowned by them; they keep the ground that is under them without hay or corn; that is no privilege. Whatsoever good or harm they do they are not to be credited to kings, save to that King who is the ruler of heaven, and sought no help in their making.'

The metre of some of the poems is the fully strict style, but most are in the simpler kind of *deibhidhe*, syllabically strict but without internal rime or regular alliteration.

And here is a sample of Lughaidh and Tadhg in fully strict style:

Ná brosd mise, a Mhic Dáire,
go laochraidh fóid fionnMháighe;
atá agaibh, madh áil daoibh,
cagail d'Íbh Táil nó a dtathaoir . . .

Ní fhéachfaid dot ór dána,
gidh dóigh led lucht combágha
nach baoghal libh as a los,
dá gclaonadh sibh an seanchas.

Dán órdha ní hé do-ní
cosnamh gach cúise adeirthí
is taosga i dTealaigh na bhFionn,
achd leabhair aosda Éirionn.

Dob fhéidir dhó re dán nglas,
gibé file is fearr eólas
fa chlár dTeamhra na dtachar
dán breaghdha do bhréagnachadh.

'Do not incite me, Mac Dáire, against the heroes of the soil
of the fair Maigue; you can have whichever you prefer for the
line of Tál, mercy or censure . . . They (*i.e.* Tadhg's adversaries)
will not consider the gold of your art, though your sympathizers
think you are safe because of it, if you pervert history. It is not
a gilded poem that can most readily defend every cause you
mention in the Hill of the Fair, but the ancient books of
Ireland. The poet with most knowledge of the land of Tara
of the frays could refute an elaborate poem by a plain one.'

From Tadhg's rejoinder:

A Lughaidh, labhram go séimh,
ná bíom go tréan ar toibhéim:
cúis inbheadhgtha nárbh fheidhm dhuibh
deilbh mh'imdheargtha gan fhachuin . . .

An fiuchadh do fiuchadh libh
lem' chéidfhreagra do chluinsin,
clódh a bhfuil d'uaill san fhiuchadh
suaill nach muir do mhíniuchadh.

Taobh re freagra ar labh adh leam
níor anais, anba an dícheall,
ní f huair grádh ná eagla th'f hos
gan fhreagra a lán nár labhras . . .

An gcéin bhias cóir ar mo chúl
ní dóigh liom cách dom chlaochlúdh,
ní taobh tollairbhe taobh ruinn,
comairghe ar aon ní iarraim.

'Ah Lughaidh, let us speak gently, let us not be strongly abusive; to insult me without reason is a cause of disquiet that were no advantage to you. The bubbling wherewith you bubbled at hearing my first rejoinder—to subdue the arrogance of that bubbling would be almost to calm the sea. You didn't stop at replying to what I had said, but, great the exertion, neither love nor fear was able to stop thee from answering much that I never said. Whilst I have right at my back, I do not expect that anyone will refuse me; to rely on me is not to rely on a broken fence; I seek protection from none.'

One of the Contention poems, a piece ascribed in some manuscripts to Robert MacArthur, in one to Flaithrí Ó Maoil Chonaire, shows a noteworthy development in metrical style, a loosening of the bonds of the *rann* or quatrain, allowing a sentence to continue from one quatrain to another instead of making each quatrain a completed statement.

O'Curry believed that 'the real object' of the Contention was 'simply to rouse and keep alive the national feeling and family pride of such of the native nobility and gentry as still continued to hold any station of rank or fortune in the country' (*Manuscript Materials of Ir. Hist.* 141). This view, which seems at least partially correct, is discussed by Father L. McKenna in his edition of the poems, Irish Texts Soc. xx, xxi. A gloomy and cynical commentary on the whole affair, anonymous in most copies, is ascribed in one manuscript to Flaithrí Ó Maoil Chonaire:

Lughaidh Tadhg 7 Torna,
ollaimh oirdhearca ár dtalaimh,
coin iad go n-iomad fheasa
ag troid fán easair fhalaimh.

'Lughaidh, Tadhg and Torna, famous poets of our land; hounds are they with much learning, wrangling over an empty dish.'[1]

In any case it remains for us a treasury of idiom, of poetic style, legendary history and tradition, however pathetic as a quasi-political enterprise it may appear now.

CONCLUSION

How shall we sum up the general literary value of *dán díreach* as a metrical form? An exotic style introduced into Ireland at the dawn of the era of letters and eventually adopted by a jealous corporation of rigid traditionalists, by whom, before the opening of the thirteenth century, it was wrought to the utmost elaboration in accordance with its own nature, and afterwards maintained in use for over four centuries. Did this work disastrously on the literary development of the nation, hindering the use and growth of a natural gift for clear and graceful prose such as is exemplified in some early narratives of our ancient legends? The fact is that we know too little about what really happened, to pass a verdict. We have undoubted evidence that simpler kinds of versification continued in use all along. Bergin[2] has shown that the stressed metres of the eighteenth century are fully Irish and have an ancient history. We have seen above a movement of the court poets themselves to 'go out into the rain', and write for the vulgar. But it was too late then to close

---

[1] 'dish': lit. 'litter; any strewn covering for a floor'. For the rendering here *cf*. RIA Dict. s.v. *esair*. But O'Grady, Cat. p. 617, is perhaps more accurate in rendering it: 'the empty kennel (i.e. when the pups of both are stolen)'.

[2] See his paper 'On the origin of Modern Irish Rhythmical Verse', in *Mélanges linguistiques offerts à M. Holger Pedersen* (Copenhagen, 1937).

the gap between schools and people in this way. It was not very seriously attempted. Even the Franciscan revivalists of the seventeenth century in their easy prose did not always discard scholastic prejudice.

Rather than reproach the poets for what they did not do, let us be grateful to them for the many delightful poems they have left us, and for what they preserved for us through their care for tradition.

II

SAGA AND MYTH IN
ANCIENT IRELAND

IRISH storytelling has always specially attracted the student of antiquity. In it he finds something unique in European tradition, a rich mass of tales depicting a West-European barbaric civilization as yet uninfluenced by the mighty sister-civilization of Graeco-Roman lands. Likewise, the lover of literature, having exhausted the possibilities of the maturer literatures of other countries, finds in Irish storytelling something to delight him from the youth of the world, before the heart had been trained to bow before the head or the imagination to be troubled by logic and reality: Cú Chulainn, abandoning his watch over the frontiers of Ulster to keep a pledged tryst with the King of Tara's wife, need fear no implied rebuke from the narrator of his deeds, and the strange impact on the human world of the spirit folk who dwell unseen by men in the hills beside them is accepted as part of an order which men as yet neither sought to understand nor rebelled against by reason of its injustice.

Though our knowledge of ancient Irish storytelling comes mainly from manuscript versions of the tales, there can be little doubt that Irish narrative tradition has on the whole been essentially oral. That this was the universal rule at least till the middle of the seventh century no scholar would deny. That it has also been the rule for two hundred years past, both in Ireland and Gaelic Scotland, where the folktale is concerned, is also an undeniable fact. Thurneysen, however, author of what will for long remain the standard treatise on ancient Irish storytelling,[1] believed that, from the eighth

---

[1] R. Thurneysen, *Die irische Helden- und Königsage*, I–II (1921). For Thurneysen's view of the relationship of manuscript and oral tradition see especially pp. 72–73. For arguments against it see *Ériu*, XVI (1952), 151–2. A more general presentation of the case for oral transmission of Irish tales will be found in *Duanaire Finn*, III (ed. G. Murphy), 189–192.

and ninth centuries on, the main body of Irish narrative tradition was propagated normally by means of manuscripts.

Now Thurneysen, in the work referred to, has undoubtedly proved that the manuscript tradition of a tale, once it had received written form, seems normally to have been carried on, in the manuscripts, independently of oral tradition, though this is not the case so universally as he would have held. As has been pointed out, however, in *Ériu*, XVI (1952), 152, the tendency of scribes to reproduce an already written text no more disproves the existence of a living oral tradition than the tendency of folklorists of the last generation to use Curtin as their source disproves the fact that a vigorous oral tradition of folktale-telling is still being carried on in Gaelic-speaking districts wholly uninfluenced by Curtin's or any other folklorist's recordings.

Perhaps a stronger argument for the literary nature of Irish story-tradition, from the eighth and ninth centuries on, is the usage of the greater part of medieval Europe. But that Irish narrative tradition was different from that of medieval Europe rather than governed by the same laws, is strongly suggested by the written texts themselves, first because in those texts 'telling' and 'hearing' stories is commonly referred to, and secondly because as a rule the stories are very imperfectly narrated in the manuscripts and not infrequently in a way that definitely suggests recording from an oral source.

The artistry of the modern Gaelic storyteller is often remarkable, and the critical spirit of his peasant audience highly developed. Professor James H. Delargy is therefore right when he suggests that the more cultivated audiences of the Irish middle ages would not 'have listened very long to the story-teller if he were to recite tales in the form in which they have come down to us.'[1] Moreover several of the best manuscript texts begin well, but tail off badly as the

[1] *The Gaelic Story-teller* (1954), 32.

story proceeds. This strange procedure can be easily explained on the hypothesis of recording from oral recitation. Everyone who has tried to record Irish folktales from peasant reciters before the introduction of recording machines has noticed the curtailment and imperfection which tend gradually to creep into the recorded narrative owing to the growing weariness of the reciter. Recorders in other countries have been acutely aware of the same phenomenon. Radlov, a collector of Tartar epic poetry, has, for instance, been quoted as follows by H. M. and Mrs. Chadwick in their *Growth of Literature*, III (1940), 180:

> In spite of all my efforts I have not succeeded in reproducing the poetry of the minstrels completely. The repeated singing of one and the same song, the slow dictation, and my frequent interruptions often dispersed the excitement which is necessary to the minstrel for good singing. He was only able to dictate in a tired and negligent way what he had produced for me a little before with fire.

And the Chadwicks themselves a few pages later (183) say that 'the weariness of the singer, and the consequent lapses of memory and flagging narrative are constantly brought home to us as we draw towards the close of Radlov's poems, which offer a striking contrast to their brilliant opening scenes'.

When we think of the well-constructed narratives which even the unlearned peasant narrator to-day can produce, and when we judge of the greater power of Old Irish storytellers by consideration of certain passages scattered through the inartistic manuscript versions of their tales which have been preserved, we can be fairly certain that the tales, as really told to assembled kings and noblemen at an ancient *óenach*, were very different from the poorly-narrated manuscript versions noted down by monastic scribes as a contribution to learning rather than to literature.

The ninth-century story of Cano son of Gartnán offers

a good example. Its opening paragraph[1] leads the reader
to expect exquisite artistry in the tale as a whole:

> Áedan son of Gabrán, and Gartnán son of Áed, were con-
> tending for the kingship of Scotland, and half the men of Scotland
> fell between them in fights and battles. Gartnán lived in Inis
> Macu Chéin.[2] That island was covered with the best buildings
> in the western part of the world. Every house on the island all
> around it, including the privy, was of strip-work laid over beams
> of red yew from peak to peak in Gartnán's time. Gartnán had
> his whole island gilded with red gold. On the arable land he had
> seven plough-teams. He had seven herds with seven score cows
> in each herd. He had fifty nets for deer, and out from the island
> were fifty nets for fishing. The fifty fish-nets had ropes from them
> over the windows of the kitchen. There was a bell at the end of
> each rope, on the rail, in front of the steward. Four men used to
> throw (?) the first-run salmon up to him. He himself in the mean-
> time drank mead upon his couch.

About page 2 of the printed text one begins to suspect that
elaborate descriptions of this sort are being hinted at rather
than recorded, and from page 3 on, the story begins to resemble a summary of incidents rather than a tale meant to
hold the interest of an audience by its artistry.

The printed text would take about half an hour to recite.
Modern folktales as told by good storytellers often take an
hour to recite, and some of them may even be spun out to
last for several sessions.[3] Moreover it is the long tale which
is most highly thought of to-day by Gaelic peasant
audiences,[4] and similar love of length has been commented
on by collectors of oral literature in other regions.[5] We
should hardly be far wrong, therefore, in conjecturing that
the Story of Cano son of Gartnán as really told in the ninth
century would have contained many elaborate passages

---

[1] K. Meyer, *Anecdota from Irish Manuscripts*, I (1907), 1. (A new edition
of the text has appeared since the above was written: *Scéla Cano meic Gartnáin*,
D. A. Binchy, Dublin Institute for Advanced Studies, 1963, J.C.)

[2] To-day Skye.   [3] J. H. Delargy, *The Gaelic Story-teller*, 21–22.
[4] *Ib.*, 34.   [5] Cf. the Chadwicks, *l.c.*, 185.

reminiscent of the opening passage just quoted, would have been much better knit than the manuscript version, and would have taken an hour or several hours to tell. Moreover, in the tales as originally told, not the opening, but some episode in the middle or end would probably have most awakened our admiration. For it is the law of oral narration that the story improves as the appreciation of the audience begins to affect the narrator.[1]

Whereas modern French story-tradition, let us say, is purely literary, and thirteenth-century French story-tradition, in so far as the reciter had derived his text from a manuscript, is essentially literary, it is unlikely that Irish story-tradition before the seventeenth century depended to any large extent upon manuscripts. Medieval Irish manuscripts would seem indeed to be related to living story-telling much as the museum to-day is related to living material culture. The manuscripts contain samples from interesting specimens of genuine storytelling, particularly from out-of-date specimens, arranged without much attention to artistic requirements, just as the museum contains samples of out-of-date furniture and household utensils arranged with a view to antiquarian instruction rather than to suit the purposes of real life.

In 1940 Domhnall Bán Ó Céileachair, a West Cork farmer, published an autobiography[2] which he had dictated to his sons and daughters, who were then school-children. In the process of correcting the script in preparation for having it printed, Domhnall Bán's wife was often present and would sometimes complain that such and such an episode had not been suitably narrated. Domhnall Bán would usually admit the defect and begin to narrate the episode orally. Had he been able, at the moment of dictating, to capture the fire and eloquence of the moment of oral

---

[1] 'The sympathy of the hearers always spurs the minstrel to new efforts of strength,' writes Radlov of Tartar epic poetry (Chadwicks, *l.c.*, 184).
[2] Domhnall Bán Ó Céileachair, *Sgéal mo Bheatha*.

narration, and had the scribes been able to record what he said, how much more excellent would that excellent autobiography have been! But such a combination was, alas, impossible. If it was impossible in the days of steel pen, paper jotter, printing press, and paper book, how much more impossible was it in the days of the *stilus*, waxed tablet, quill pen, and vellum codex! When, therefore, we form a picture of the orally narrated Irish tale as something immeasurably superior to the suggestions of it a monastic scribe has recorded, we are not creating a figment of the imagination, we are merely restoring to the corpse buried in a manuscript the soul that once animated it.

Sgéalaighe (as the word for storyteller is spelt in Modern Irish) to-day awakens thoughts of an unlettered fisherman or farmer telling folktales by a cottage fireside. To the ninth-century author of the Exile of the Sons of Uisliu,[1] however, or to the late-twelfth-century author of the poem on Gréssach, the Túath Dé Danann storyteller, contained in the fourteenth-century Book of Uí Maine,[2] the word *scélaige* would have had more aristocratic associations. Feidlimid mac Daill, Conchobar's pre-Christian *scélaige* in the Exile of the Sons of Uisliu, is represented for instance, as entertaining princes in his house and as having a daughter, Deirdre, who was a fitting consort for a king. Indeed, from the differences observable between different genres of storytelling, from references in literary texts to storytellers of different ranks in society, and from analogy with the first steps of an ascending scale still to be noticed in Gaelic-speaking districts,[3] it may be concluded that in ancient Ireland a whole hierarchy of storytellers existed, ranging from the humble teller of folktales to the *fili*, who as well as being a learned poet, master of *senchus* (history) and *dinnshenchus* (placelore), had been trained to narrate 'the chief stories of Ireland to kings, lords,

---

[1] V. Hull, *Longes Mac n-Uislenn* (1949), 43 and 60, §1.
[2] Facsimile, 157a8 (=216a8).
[3] *Duanaire Finn*, III (ed. G. Murphy), xxxvii–xxxix, 189–192.

and noblemen'.[1] From a text in eighth-century Irish, for example,[2] we learn that Mongán son of Fiachna, an East Ulster king who died about A.D. 625, was told a story by his *fili*, Forgoll, every winter night from *Samuin* to *Beltaine* (1st November to 1st May).

Irish scribes of all periods have tended to record in their manuscripts only the lore of whatever happened to be the most learned class of their day. We may take it, therefore, that the type of storytelling which we see imperfectly reflected in medieval manuscripts is on the whole that of the *fili*, who in real life probably told his tales at their best in the *óenaige* (fairs), where, under the patronage of kings and the sanction of age-old custom, the arts of early Ireland seem to have received their fullest expression.[3]

Twelfth-century *filid* divided the tales they told into *prím-scéla* and *fo-scéla*, main tales and subsidiary tales; and, though the numbers are hardly to be taken as exact, they claimed to know in all seven times fifty (350) tales, of which five fifties (250) were main tales, and two fifties (100) subsidiary tales. Comparatively few of the tales have been preserved till the present day, but two long lists of the titles of main tales, representing perhaps the repertory of tenth-century *filid*, with some eleventh and twelfth-century additions, are extant to-day, as well as a third similar summary list.[4] In the lists, the tales are classified by the first words of their titles into *Togla* (destructions), *Tána* (cattle-raids), *Tochmarca* (wooings), *Catha* (battles), *Uatha* (caves),[5]

---

[1] *Is hi dano foglaim na hochtmaide bliadna . . . ocus din[n]shenchus ocus primscéla Hérend olchena fria naisnéis do ríghaib ocus flaithib ocus dagdhoínib* (The matter learnt in the eighth year [of a poet's training] consisted of . . . and placelore and the chief stories of Ireland also, to narrate them to kings and lords and noblemen), *Mittelirische Verslehren*, II, §91, ed. Thurneysen in Stokes and Windisch's *Irische Texte*, III (1891), 50.

[2] K. Meyer, *Voyage of Bran*, I (1895), 45–46. Cf. Thurneysen, *Heldensage* (1912), 67.

[3] *Studies*, March 1940, 22–23.   [4] Thurneysen, *op. cit.*, 21–24.

[5] Cf. Early Modern *fuathacha* 'holes (in the ground)', *Regimen na Sláinte* (*Regimen Sanitatis Magnini Mediolanensis*), ed. S. Ó Ceithearnaigh, II,

Immrama (voyages), *Aite* (deaths), *Fessa* (feasts), *Forbasa* (sieges), *Echtrai* (adventure-journeys), *Aitheda* (elopements), *Airgne* (slaughters), *Tomadmann* (eruptions), *Slúagaid* (expeditions), *Tochomlada* (immigrations), *Físi* (visions), and *Serca* (love-tales). Modern scholars, however, prefer to classify the stories partly according to their subject-matter and partly according to their spirit into Mythological tales, Heroic tales, King tales, Finn tales, and Romantic tales.

In this section an attempt will be made to describe the Mythological tales, the Heroic tales, and the King tales. Finn tales and Romantic tales received their greatest development after the Old and Middle Irish periods.[1] They will therefore be treated of separately under the title The Ossianic Lore and Romantic Tales of Medieval Ireland.

MYTHOLOGICAL TALES

From the oldest period of Irish tradition down to the present day Irish storytellers speak currently of a spirit folk living close to human beings, but normally concealed from them. They are the *áes síde* of Old Irish tradition, known in spoken Irish as the *slúagh sídhe* (*síodh*-host), *slúagh aérach* (airy host), *bunadh na gcnoc* (hill folk), *daoine maithe* (good people), etc., and in English as the fairies. From ancient times they have been looked upon as dwelling either in certain hills called *sídi* (Modern Irish *sídhe* or *síodha*, from which conception comes their name *áes síde*, 'people of the *sídi*'), or in far-away islands, or beneath the waters of the sea or of lakes. To the learned in Gaelic Ireland the *áes síde* were known as *Túatha Dé Donann* (later *Danann*), which originally meant the Peoples of the Goddess Donu.[2]

---

[1] Old Irish, c.600–c.900; Middle Irish, c.900–c.1200; Early Modern Irish, c.1200–c.1650.

[2] See *Duanaire Finn*, III, 208–210.

5665, 5834. The *Uatha*, most of which are wholly lost, seem to refer to incidents which took place in famous caves.

When in poetic and storytelling mood even the learned made little or no attempt to conceal the fact that the Túatha Dé Donann were a spirit folk. When in historical mood, however, they euhemerized them into a human race, skilled in magic, who once occupied Ireland but were defeated by the invading *Goídil* or Gaels. Stories which introduce the *des síde* or Túatha Dé Donann as principal actors are to-day known as Mythological tales, for to the modern scholar it is clear that the Túatha Dé Donann and *des síde* were the gods of pagan Ireland surrounded by the lesser divinities and spirits over whom they ruled. Many of the chief persons among them are identifiable with Celtic gods known to us from other sources: *Lug*, for instance, with the god who gave his name to Lyons (Lugudunum), Laon, Leyden, and other continental towns;[1] and *Núadu* with the *Nodons* (or *Nodens*) who was worshipped in a Romano-British temple at Lydney Park in Gloucestershire.[2] The divine nature of others among them is guaranteed by ancient Irish tradition: thus Cormac, king and bishop of Cashel about the year 900, states in his Glossary that Manannán was god of the sea (*inde Scotti et Brittones eum deum vocaverunt maris*); and the same writer suggests the Dagda's divinity by saying that the Dagda's daughter Brigit, patroness of poetry, was adored as a goddess.[3] Indeed the Dagda's name, which originally would have meant 'good god', in itself suggests his godhood, while the fact that his daughter Brigit, patroness of poetry, had two sisters, also called Brigit and patronesses respectively of law and smithcraft, reminds one of the tendency of the Gallic Celts to present their divinities in triadic form.[4] Moreover the background and atmosphere of

---

[1] *l.c.*, lxxiv–lxxvi.

[2] A. C. L. Brown, *The Origin of the Grail Legend* (1943), 146; R. A. S. Macalister, *Lebor Gabála Érenn*, IV (1941), 97–98.

[3] There can be little doubt that she is the same as the *dea Brigantia* of Roman Britain: cf. Dottin, *Religion des Celtes* (1908), 20, and Vendryes, *La Religion des Celtes* (1948), 272.

[4] Dottin, *l.c.*, 25.

the tales, redolent of marvel, preternatural power and strange loveliness, are such as one would expect in a mythological cycle. In this respect the Irish mythological tales remind one of the Welsh *Mabinogion*, in which many Túatha Dé Donann names occur in Welsh form—*Donu* as *Don*,[1] *Mac ind Óc* as *Mabon*,[2] *Lug* as *Lleu*, *Núadu* as *Nudd*, *Manannán* as *Manawydan*, *Goibniu* as *Govannon*—suggesting that the spirit and some of the characters of the two groups of tales go back to the primitive paganism once shared by these two Celtic peoples.

In tales of the Irish Mythological cycle we may therefore expect to find much of the mythology of the primitive Celts. It is to be noted, however, that mythology, largely the creation of poets and storytellers, gives little information concerning the essential elements of a people's religion. From what Homer tells us of the loves and enmities of the Olympians ruled over by Zeus we could, for instance, learn but little of religious rites such as the Eleusinian mysteries and of the various feasts and sacrifices by which the Athenian citizen in the fifth century B.C. hoped to ensure the well-being of himself and his city. Greek myths as preserved for us by Roman poets are still further divorced from religion understood in the true sense of the word. Many Irish mythological tales have survived through the Christian ages by reason of their value as stories; but, as remembered by the Christian Irish, they throw no more light on ancient Celtic religion than the Roman versions of Greek myths, unaided by Greek religious monuments, would throw on ancient Greek religion. Neglect of this consideration has led to several unjustified conclusions concerning primitive Irish religion. E. J. Gwynn,[3] for instance, believed that the absence of 'evidence of ritual, or worship or prayer or

---

[1] *Duanaire Finn*, III, lxxxiii, 208–210, 447.
[2] T. F. O'Rahilly, *The Goidels and their Predecessors* (1935), 38.
[3] See pp. 54 and 55 of *The Church of Ireland, A.D. 432–1932* (Report of the Church of Ireland Conference . . . 1932).

sacrifice', indicated a religion among the Gaels 'unworthy of their general level of culture', and A. G. van Hamel[1] that, where other peoples gave religious cult to gods, the Celts used to tell what he calls Exemplary Myths concerning protection of the land in past time by Heroes, these Exemplary Myths being intended partly to teach kings how to carry out their task of actually protecting the land in the present, partly to bring about, by the mere recitation of them, recurrence of the victories and blessings which were the Heroes' lot. Avoiding similar rash conclusions, we shall in this section discuss the Mythological tales for their story value only, making little or no attempt to relate them to the fundamental religious beliefs and practices of the pagan Celts.

Of all the Mythological tales that entitled *Cath Maige Tuired*, the Battle of Moytirra,[2] is of greatest interest to students of Irish mythology, for in it almost the whole Irish

[1] In his *Aspects of Celtic Mythology* (1934). For criticism of Van Hamel's opinions see *Duanaire Finn*, III, 213–217.

[2] Moytirra (East and West) are two townlands near Lough Arrow, Co. Sligo. The tale discussed in the present section was originally referred to simply as *Cath Maige Tuired*. Later it is sometimes called *Cath Dédenach Maige Tuired* ('The Last Battle of M. T.), or *Cath Tánaiste Maige Tuired* ('The Second Battle of M. T.), and later still *Cath Maighe Tuireadh Thúaidh* ('The Battle of Northern M. T.). These names are used to distinguish it from another battle, in which, according to eleventh-century historical doctrine, the Túatha Dé Danann won Ireland from the Fir Bolg, twenty-seven years before defeating the Fomoiri in the more famous battle here under considera- tion. The battle against the Fir Bolg is often called *Cét-chath Maige Tuired* ('The First Battle of M. T.). To distinguish it still more clearly from the more famous battle with the Fomoiri it was ultimately decided that it was fought at a different 'plain of pillars' near Cong, Co. Mayo, about fifty miles south- west of the original Moytirra: this explains the late names *Cath Maighe Tuireadh Cunga* ('The Battle of M. T. of Cong), and *Cath Maighe Tuireadh Theas* ('The Battle of Southern M. T.).

For the location of *Mag Tuired* ('Plain of Pillars', now called Moytirra), and for references to the names given the two battles, see T. F. O'Rahilly, *Early Ir. Hist. and Mythol.* (1946), 388–390. For arguments against T. F. O'Rahilly's thesis that 'the story of the first battle of Mag Tuired was in existence before that of the second, to which it served as model', see *Éigse*, VII (1954), 191 sq.

pantheon appears. Its theme, a battle in which the Túatha Dé Donann defeat the Fomoiri, is reminiscent of Greek traditions concerning the defeat inflicted on Cronus and his Titans by Zeus and the Olympian gods, or of Scandinavian traditions concerning wars between Aesir and Vanir.

The Fomoiri are normally pictured as unpleasant spirits dwelling overseas to the north of Ireland. There is a vagueness, however, in Irish tradition concerning them which is in marked contrast with the clear characterization and wealth of detail about individuals which has been handed down concerning the Túatha Dé Donann. Indeed the vagueness is such that it has permitted so great an expert as T. F. O'Rahilly to suggest that between the Fomoiri and the Túatha Dé 'there is at bottom no real distinction'.[1] Greek tradition concerning the Titans, however, when compared with Greek tradition concerning the Olympian gods, is marked by a similar vagueness. Moreover the Fomoiri, like the Titans, are in Irish tradition consistently pictured in an unfavourable light, and when they are specifically referred to as Fomoiri they are as consistently opposed to the Túatha Dé as the Greek Titans are to the Olympian gods. It would seem therefore that a similar contrast between two groups of spirits, and traditions of a battle between them, go back to the days of primitive Indo-European unity and are not of such late origin as O'Rahilly would have had us believe.

Cath Maige Tuired is named in the three tale-lists mentioned *supra* (p. 103) as a tale that a *fili* should be able to tell. An idea of how it was told at different periods may be gained from reading the three extant manuscript tales connected with it.

The oldest of these is entitled *Cath Maige Turedh ocus Genemain Bres Meic Elathain ocus a Ríghe*, 'The Battle of Moytirra, and the Birth of Bres Son of Elathan and His Reign'. It is preserved in the sixteenth-century British Museum manuscript, Harley 5280, f. 63 sq., and has been

---

[1] O'Rahilly, *l.c.*, 524.

edited with a translation by Stokes, RC, XII, 56 sq. Omissions in Stokes' edition have been supplied by Thurneysen, ZCP, XII, 401 sq. It would seem to be a composite work put together by an eleventh or twelfth-century redactor mainly from ninth-century material.

The second is entitled *Do Chath Mhuighe Tuireadh*, 'Concerning the Battle of Moytirra'. It is preserved in the seventeenth-century Royal Irish Academy manuscript, 24 P 9, f. 65 sq., and has been edited in booklet form by Brian Ó Cuív (1945). It deals with the immediate preparations for the battle and the battle itself, omitting the description of Bres's tyranny over the Túatha Dé and the coming of their saviour, Lug, described in the introductory portion of the older text. But the first paragraph of this second text clearly implies knowledge on the part of the reader of something corresponding to that introduction. This second manuscript tale was first written down probably in the thirteenth century. While in general theme it agrees with the older text, in style and in detail it is quite independent of it.

The third manuscript tale is entitled *Oidheadh Chloinne Tuireann*, 'The Death of the Children of Tuireann', and is preserved in many eighteenth- and nineteenth-century manuscripts. It describes the coming of Lug in a form completely different from that given in the old text and, in addition as its main theme, the obtaining by the three sons of Tuireann, at Lug's behest, of magic articles to be used by him in the battle. It ends with an account of the death of the three sons of Tuireann, before the battle, as the result of wounds received by them in fulfilling their task. *Oidheadh Chloinne Tuireann* was certainly in existence in the sixteenth century,[1] and the main elements of it are all mentioned in some form or other between the eleventh and late fourteenth centuries.[2] As known to us from eighteenth- and nineteenth-

---

[1] *Éigse*, IV, 249.
[2] Flower, *Catalogue*, II, 348–349; O'Rahilly, *Early Ir. Hist. and Mythol.*, 308–317.

century manuscripts it would seem to represent late scribes' recensions of a text that was probably written down in a substantially similar form in the fourteenth century.[1]

The existence of these three manuscript tales, differing greatly from one another even when they describe the same incidents, and the existence of many different accounts of various incidents connected with the battle spread widely through the literature of all periods,[2] suggest both that *Cath Maige Tuired* was always a popular story and that the tradition of it was essentially oral, unified where the main theme was concerned, but, like all oral tradition, constantly varying in the manner of presentation of that theme and in the particular incidents introduced into it.

The oldest of these three manuscript tales is the longest and most interesting. Nevertheless it is probably the least like any of the living methods of telling the story current at any period; for its juxtaposition of Old Irish and Middle Irish matter and its tendency to record stray scraps of lore about the characters mentioned, rather than to concentrate on episodes essential to the theme, remind one forcibly of the museum type of arrangement, already referred to on p. 101, which is so common in manuscripts texts of our older saga-tradition. Some passages, however, particularly that which narrates the coming of Lug (the Samildánach) from *Emain Ablach* ('Emain of the Apple-trees'—the Arthurian Avalon), when the Túatha Dé were most in need of him, may be used to form an idea of the artistry which doubtless would have characterized the whole story as told at a ninth-century *óenach*:

The doorkeeper saw an unknown troop approaching him. A fair and shapely warrior, with a king's trappings was in the forefront of that band. They bade the doorkeeper to announce in Tara that they had come. 'Who is here?' said the doorkeeper. 'Here is Lug of the fierce combats, son of Cían son of Dían Cécht, and of Ethniu daughter of Balar; he is the fosterson

---

[1] Cf. O'Rahilly, *l.c.*, 312, n.2.   [2] See *Éigse*, VII, 196, n.3.

of Talann, daughter of Magmór king of Spain, and of Echaid
the Rough son of Duí.'

The doorkeeper asked the Samildánach:[1] 'What art dost thou
practice? For no one without an art enters Tara.' 'Question me,'
he said: 'I am a wright.' The doorkeeper answered: 'We need
no wright. We have a wright already, Luchta son of Lúachaid.'
He said: 'Question me, doorkeeper: I am a smith.' The doorkeeper answered him: 'We have a smith already, Colum
Cúailleinech of the three new processes.' He said: 'Question me:
I am a champion.' The doorkeeper answered: 'We need thee not.
We have a champion already, Ogma son of Ethliu.' He said
again: 'Question me: I am a harper.' 'We need thee not. We
have a harper already, Abcán son of Bicelmos whom the Men
of the Three Gods entertained in *síd*-mounds.' He said: 'Question
me: I am a warrior.' The doorkeeper answered: 'We need thee
not. We have a warrior already Bresal Echarlam son of Echu
Báethlám.' Then he said: 'Question me, doorkeeper: I am a
poet and historian.' 'We need thee not: we have a poet and
historian already, Én son of Ethoman.' He said: 'Question me:
I am a sorcerer.' 'We need thee not. We have sorcerers already;
our wizards and men of power are many.' He said: 'Question me:
I am a leech.' 'We need thee not. As leech we already have
Dían Cécht.' 'Question me,' said he: 'I am a cupbearer.' 'We
need thee not. We already have cupbearers, Delt and Drúcht
and Daithe, Taí and Talam and Trog, Glé and Glan and
Glése.' He said: 'Question me: I am a good metal-worker.'
'We need thee not: we already have a metal-worker, Credne
the Metal-worker.' He spoke again saying: 'Ask the king
whether he has one single man who possesses all these arts,
and if he has I shall not enter Tara.'

The doorkeeper went into the palace and declared all to
the king. 'A warrior has come before the garth,' said he, 'called
Samildánach; and that one man possesses all the arts practised by
thy household so that he is the man of each and every art.'
'Let him into the garth,' said Núadu; 'for his like has never
before come to this fortress.'

[1] *Ildánach* means 'possessing many crafts'. The prefix *sam*, which occurs
before other adjectives, is taken by Stokes (RC, XII, 123) to mean 'together,
at the same time'.

Then the doorkeeper let Lug pass him, and he went into the fortress and sat in the sage's seat for he was a sage in every art.[1]

A sentence describing Lug's winning a game of *fidchell*,[2] which seems out of place in the context, and another sentence on the origin of that game, which is certainly due to a late glossator, have been omitted in the above citation. It is unlikely that anything corresponding to either sentence would have been heard in the story as told in the ninth century. It will be noticed too that the doorkeeper knows that Lug is called the Samildánach, though that name had not been given him in the conversation upon which his knowledge of the stranger's identity is supposed to be based. Such a lapse from the canons of good storytelling would hardly have occurred in a genuine telling of the tale.

Cath Maige Tuired gives us more information about individual members of the ancient Irish pantheon than any other single tale of the mythological cycle. The otherworld atmosphere which gives its special beauty to that cycle is, however, better illustrated in other tales, such as the ninth-century *Tochmarc Étaíne* or 'Wooing of Étaín', which tells how Étaín, wooed and won by Midir in the otherworld, was transformed into a brilliantly-coloured fly by her rival Fúamnach, who blew her into this world, where, swallowed in a drink by an Ulster queen, she was reborn as a human. Wooed once more in human shape by the king of Tara, she was ultimately won back to the otherworld by Midir as

---

[1] RC, XII, 74–78 (§§53–71). A still more artistic telling of this episode is to be found in a poem beginning *Mór ar bhfearg riot, a rí Saxon* ('Great is our wrath against thee, King of England'), written to honour Maurice FitzMaurice, second earl of Desmond, in the middle of the fourteenth century. The author of the poem, Gofraidh Fionn Ó Dálaigh, doubtless following the oral tradition of his day, makes Lug concentrate on his magic or acrobatic arts, such as 'leaping on a bubble without breaking it'. Though the doorkeeper in Gofraidh's poem is ordered by the Túatha Dé to admit Lug, Lug, to avoid breaking the *geis* or 'taboo' which forbade the fortress of Tara to be opened before sunrise, leaped over the rampart.

[2] The later Irish, including the author of this gloss, identified *fidchell*, a native board-game, with chess (see *Éigse*, V, 25).

the result of a rash stake made by the king in a game of *fidchell*.

Many tales, often with the word *Echtra*, 'adventure-journey', in their title, tell of the journeys of human beings to the otherworld. They tend to have a peculiar beauty by reason of the descriptions contained in them of the land 'where there is nought but truth, where there is neither age, nor decay, nor gloom, nor sadness, nor envy, nor jealousy, nor hate, nor pride'.[1] Though essentially mythological, they may be loosely connected with any cycle by reason of their human hero. Thus *Seirglige Con Culainn ocus Óenét Emire*, 'Cú Chulainn's Wasting Sickness and Emer's Only Jealousy', extant in a composite version which includes ninth-century and eleventh-century strata, might, by reason of the presence in it of Cú Chulainn, be classified with the Heroic tales. It tells of the love-sickness induced in Cú Chulainn by Fann, wife of Manannán, and Cú Chulainn's resultant journey to her court. This fairy mistress type of tale is still popular in Irish folklore.

Closely allied to the *Echtrai* are the *Immrama* or 'Voyages'. In them the otherworld is pictured as situated on islands in the western ocean. The earliest of them, the eighth-century *Immram Brain*, or 'Voyage of Bran', is essentially pagan in character. But by the ninth century the *Immrama* had been adapted to suit a Christian outlook and may describe the magic islands visited by Christian monks or penitents. On one of these Christianized *Immrama*, the ninth-century *Immram Máile Dúin*, or 'Voyage of Máel Dúin', a late-ninth- or early-tenth-century Irish Latinist modelled his *Navigatio Brendani*, which, translated into many continental languages, became one of the most popular stories of the Middle Ages and played an important part in inspiring those real voyages which culminated in the discovery of America.

[1] *Echtra Chormaic i dTír Tairngire*, 'Cormac's Journey to the Land of Promise' (Stokes, *Irische Texte*, III, 1891, 193, 212, late twelfth century).

TALES OF THE HEROIC AGE

The Irish Mythological tales, and the Finn tales, which are closely related to them, are of special interest to students of the Welsh Mabinogion and the continental Arthurian tales; for, owing to the conservatism of Irish tradition, the Celtic mythological themes and motifs which are common to them all are often preserved in a more primitive form in the Irish tales. Tales of the Heroic cycle are of interest for a different reason. They preserve a spirit and tradition which but for them would have been lost to Europe. For, while a spirit akin to that of the Irish Mythological cycle has become part of the general tradition of European literature through the medium of the French Arthurian cycle, the Irish Heroic cycle is unique in being the only branch of European literature which has preserved something of the warrior spirit and tradition of the ancient Celts as known to writers of classical antiquity. It is in Greek epic literature rather than in medieval romantic literature that the Irish Heroic tales find their closest parallels.

H. M. Chadwick in his *Heroic Age*, and later in various chapters of *The Growth of Literature*, written by him in collaboration with his wife, Mrs. N. K. Chadwick, has pointed out that a type of literature commonly described as Heroic is to be found in many languages. While in style it may vary from the poetic perfection of the Greek *Iliad* to the prose ornamented with speech-poetry and 'rhetorics'[1] in which the Irish *Táin Bó Cúailnge* is presented, in matter and in the structure of its narrative it is almost everywhere the same. Heroic literature is aristocratic in outlook. As virtues it recognises loyalty, prowess, and fulfilment of one's word. Boasting, provided that the boast be equalled by the deed, is not considered a fault. It idealizes its heroes, yet remains fundamentally realistic: those heroes are made of flesh and

---

[1] Utterances of druids or heroes in obscurely worded alliterative prose, often with archaic or artificial word-order.

blood; their success or failure depends more on character and action than on accident or magic, though fate and the gods may be regarded as inscrutable yet necessary factors in life. War is the profession of the princes of whom it treats, a type of war which is direct and straightforward, almost devoid of strategy, and commonly decided by the personal prowess of leaders. Description of the ceremony of court life, of the interior of palaces, and of the ornament of clothes and weapons, is universal in heroic literature.

Chadwick has identified some of the central figures of Teutonic heroic literature with barbarian leaders mentioned by historians of the later Roman Empire. In his *Heroic Age* he had shown that the heroic poetry of the Jugoslavs is about persons of whose historic existence there can be no doubt, and that at least the material civilization of the *Iliad* corresponds to a historical reality revealed by archaeologists in the course of the last century. He concluded that heroic literature is to some extent based on history. In *The Growth of Literature* he and Mrs. Chadwick have added to the evidence for the historical occurrence of genuine Heroic Ages. Where there is heroic literature, it may therefore reasonably be inferred that a Heroic Age preceded it, and that the general traits of that Age, perhaps even some of its persons, are presented to us in that literature.

The traditions of the Irish Heroic Age centre on a period in which the *Ulaid* or 'Ulidians' were predominant in Ulster and had their capital at Emain Macha, now Navan Fort near the modern Armagh. That period must therefore certainly be anterior to the early fifth century of our era, which is the latest date to which the destruction of Emain Macha and the confinement of the Ulidians to east Co. Down by the Tara dynasty can be assigned.[1] But the type of civilization described in the tales points in fact to a much earlier century. The Ulidian warriors, for instance, are consistently pictured as fighting from chariots, an early

[1] T. F. O'Rahilly, *Early Ir. Hist. and Mythol.*, 228 sq.

mode of fighting which is not normally attributed to the warriors depicted in any other Irish group of tales, but which still survived among British Celts in the first century before Christ.[1] The tradition of the Ulidian tales may therefore be provisionally regarded as being based on a real Heroic Age which existed among the Ulidians of Emain Macha perhaps about the first century before Christ.

The Chadwicks draw particular attention to the successful raiding by barbarians of a higher civilization on the borders of which they live as a factor in producing Heroic Ages. Dr. Arnold Toynbee in his *Study of History* also treats of this factor, and in addition discusses the importance of a barbarian migration, which normally coincides with it.[2] What migration, however, or what juxtaposition of a higher and lower culture, or what similar factor was responsible for the development of the Ulidian Heroic Age can hardly be discovered in the present state of our knowledge of Irish prehistory.

The warriors of the Ulidian cycle of tales are pictured as ruled over by Conchobar mac Nessa, king of Emain, and as fighting mainly on the Meath-Ulster border. The chief hero among them is Cú Chulainn, the Achilles of Ireland, who deliberately prefers for his fate a short life and long fame to long life and little fame.[3] One or other of two similar destinies had awaited Achilles, who by deciding to fight on at Troy tacitly chose in the same way as Cú Chulainn.[4]

The central tale of the cycle is *Táin Bó Cúailnge* (The Cattle-spoil of Cooley). It tells how Cú Chulainn (The Hound of Culann), while still a youth, held up an army of Connacht invaders while awaiting the arrival of the other Ulidians, who were perforce inactive because of a strange

[1] E. Windisch, *Die altirisch Heldensage Táin Bó Cúalnge* (1905), xii sq.; H. D'Arbois de Jubainville, *Cours de Littérature Celtique*, VI.

[2] I, 92 sq.; II, 94 sq., 346, 356; V, 234 sq., 252. The volume in which Dr. Toynbee treats specifically of Heroic Ages had not been published when this work was in preparation.

[3] TBC, 550–572.   [4] *Iliad*, I, 416; IX, 411–415.

illness which used to attack them periodically, the *ces noínden* or 'nine-days illness', traced by modern anthropologists to a primitive couvade ceremony. After the first injury inflicted by Cú Chulainn on the Connacht army, their king Ailill, husband of the more famous and forceful Medb, asks the exiled Ulidian Fergus, who is guiding the invaders, 'What manner of man is this Ulster Hound of whom we have heard?' This question enables the narrator, without spoiling the unity of the whole, to work in a delightful account of Cú Chulainn's *mac-gnímrada* or 'boyhood deeds'.

Among the many concepts in the Irish *Táin* which seem to go back to primitive Indo-European beliefs reflected also in the Greek *Iliad* are the *lúan* (or *lón*) *láith*, 'champion's light' (also *lón gaile*, 'light of valour'), which plays around Cú Chulainn's head in battle,[1] the rising up of rivers to protect Cooley against the Connacht army,[2] and the occasional appearance of gods to help or oppose warriors in battle.[3]

Two main versions of *Táin Bó Cúailgne* have come down to us, a mainly Old Irish version, based on ninth-century oral tellings of the tale, and a Middle Irish version, known as the Book of Leinster version,[4] which seems to be an almost purely literary composition based on the manuscript form of

---

[1] TBC, 59, 1956; cf. *Aided Con Culainn*, 'The Death of Cú Chulainn' (RC, III, 177, 131); etc. In the *Iliad* V, 4–7, XVIII, 206–227, similar divine lights shine from the heads of Diomedes and Achilles. The Roman centurion, who, according to L. Annaeus Florus (c. A.D. 130), struck terror into the Moesi by carrying a flaming brazier on his helmet, was doubtless aware of this barbarian belief (I. Zwicker, *Fontes Religionis Celticae*, 71–72).

[2] TBC, 205, 886, 905, 910, 1035. Cf. the rising of the Scamander against Achilles to save the Trojans, *Iliad*, XXI, 234 sq. According to modern Munster folk-tradition certain rivers used to grow small to enable men of noble blood to cross them: see D. Ó Cróinín, *Dánta Árd-teistiméireachta 1949–50* (1949), p. 56 (note on line 89 of *Caoineadh Airt Uí Laoghaire*). In Irish hagiography the river Brosnach rises against the King of Tara and his army at St. Cíarán's request (C. Plummer, *Vitae Sanctorum Hiberniae*, I, 225, Vita Sancti Ciarani de Saigir, §xviii).

[3] TBC, 1713–1757, 1805. *Iliad*, passim.

[4] Ed. E. Windisch, *op. cit.*

the mainly Old Irish version. This Middle Irish version was probably first written about the year 1100, and is preserved in the Book of Leinster, which was compiled about the year 1160. It also appears with various modernizations in several later manuscripts, and though in style it is less natural and direct than the mainly Old Irish version, its unity, fullness, and freedom from contradiction make it the version to-day preferred by poets and retellers of the story.

The mainly Old Irish version,[1] according to Thurneysen's masterly analysis of it in his *Irische Helden- und Königsage,* 96 sq., seems to consist of two Old Irish texts first written down in the early ninth century and, in the eleventh century, clumsily joined together by a compiler. This compiler added certain episodes told in the Middle Irish of his day, of which the most famous is *Comrac Fir Diad* (The Fight with Fer Diad), which tells how Cú Chulainn slew in single combat his friend Fer Diad, who was one of the Connacht champions. The compilation is preserved, incomplete, in *Lebor na hUidre* (The Book of the Dun Cow), which was written at Clonmacnois about the year 1100, and also, with different lacunae, in the fourteenth-century Yellow Book of Lecan. The Old Irish portions of the compilation are pleasingly straightforward in style, but the whole work particularly towards the end, seems to be a collection of notes rather than an attempt to record the story as really told. It is marred by the inclusion of doublets of certain episodes, and even by contradictions, such as the death of Findabair, daughter of Ailill and Medb, at line 2928, and her marriage to Cú Chulainn, at line 3682, as the result of the peace made by Ailill and Medb with the Ulidians.

Fled Bricrenn (Bricriu's Feast) and *Scéla Mucce Meic Dá Thó* (The Story of Mac Dá Thó's Pig) are the other two stories which definitely mark the Ulidian cycle as a Heroic cycle in the sense in which the Chadwicks understand that

[1] Ed. J. Strachan and J. G. O'Keeffe, *The Táin Bó Cúailnge from the Yellow Book of Lecan with Variant Readings from the Leborna h Uidre* (1912).

word. Both tell of combats at feasts, following wordy argument between rival warriors, such as Posidonius Apamensis (c.135–c.50 B.C.) assures us used really to occur among the continental Celts of his day.[1]

In one of the tale-lists mentioned on p. 103, the title of the first of these stories is given as *Feis Tige Bricrenn* (The Feast of Bricriu's House). In the oldest manuscript version, that in *Lebor na hUidre*, transcribed about A.D. 1100, it is entitled *Fled Bricrend ocus in Curathmír Emna Macha, ocus in Bríatharchath ban Ulad, ocus Tochim Ulad do Chrúachnaib Aí, ocus Cennach ind Rúanada i nEmain Macha* (Bricriu's Feast and the Emain Macha Champion's Portion, and the Word-Combat of the Ulsterwomen, and the Ulstermen's Journey to Crúachain Aí, and the Warrior's Bargain in Emain Macha). This long title indicated the main episodes of the story: (1) the feast prepared by Bricriu, a well-known trouble-maker; (2) the rivalry between Loíguire Búadach, Conall Cernach, and Cú Chulainn as to who will be awarded the portion reserved for the best champion;[2] (3) the corresponding word-combat between their wives for precedence; (4) the journey to Crúachain Aí in Connacht to have the warriors' claims judged by Ailill and Medb, their testing there in combat with magic cats and the indication given by Medb that she has judged Cú Chulainn the best warrior of the three, followed by their subsequent testing in Cú Roí's palace in west Munster by other magic beings and the definite awarding by Cú Roí of the champion's portion to Cú Chulainn; (5) Cú Roí's subsequent visit to Emain Macha to make the justice of his award evident to all by means of *Cennach ind Rúanada* (The Warrior's Bargain).

None of the extant manuscripts, as Thurneysen has

---

[1] Zwicker, *l.c.* 17.

[2] In the *Iliad* (VII, 321) Agamemnon at the evening meal honours Aias for his combat with Hector by giving him 'long back-pieces' carved from a five-year-old bull which had been sacrificed. This may be compared with 'the rich piece of roast sirloin that had been given Menelaus as the portion of honour' in *Odyssey*, IV (Rieu's translation, 1945, p. 64).

pointed out (*Heldensage*, 447 sq.), preserves for us a complete text, but by use of them all a version of the story as told in the eighth or early ninth century may be restored.[1]

Classical scholars are familiar with the description of Priam's house in Book VI of the *Iliad* (ll. 243–250):

> This magnificent house was fronted with marble colonnades, and in the main building behind there were fifty apartments of polished stone, adjoining each other, where Priam's sons slept with their wives. His daughters had separate quarters, on the other side of the courtyard, where twelve adjoining bedrooms had been built for them, of polished stone, and well roofed in. Priam's sons-in-law slept with their loving wives in these.[2]

The description of the house built by Bricriu, with which *Fled Bricrenn* opens, shows the same interest in the palaces of heroes. Instead of Greek construction in marble and polished stone, we naturally, however, find the native Irish use of wood, while in literary style the sobriety and restraint of the Greek is replaced by Celtic imaginative exuberance:

> Bricriu of the Bitter Tongue had a great feast ready for Conchobar mac Nessa and all the Ulidians. He was a whole year preparing for the feast. He had made an elaborate house for the serving of the feast. That house had been constructed by Bricriu in Dún Rudraige on the model of the Branch-red palace at Emain Macha; but it excelled all houses of its day in material and artifice, in beauty and architecture, in pillars and frontals, in splendour and richness, in grace and nobility, in railings and door-frames.
>
> Now this house had been made according to the plan of the Tech Midchúarta.[3] It had nine cubicles from fire to wall: each bronze frontal was thirty feet in height and was overlaid with gold; and a royal cubicle had been constructed for Conchobar in the front of that palace higher than all its other cubicles.

---

[1] An edition based on all the manuscript texts was published by Henderson in 1899 as Vol. II of the Irish Text Society's series. For comment and indication of the interpolated portions, see Thurneysen, *l.c.*

[2] E. V. Rieu's translation (1950), 123–124.

[3] The banqueting hall at Tara.

Conchobar's cubicle was decorated with carbuncles and every other sort of precious gem. It shone with gold and silver and carbuncle and colours from many lands, so that in it night was as bright as day. The twelve compartments of the twelve Ulidian chariot-warriors had been constructed around Conchobar's. Moreover the artifice displayed was equalled by the quality of the material which had been brought to make the house. A wagon-team had been employed to bring each post, and seven of Ulster's men of might to fix every board, and thirty of Ireland's leading craftsmen to make the house and arrange it.

A sun-room belonging to Bricriu himself had been made on a level with Conchobar's and the champions' cubicles. And that sun-room had been fashioned with specially marvellous ornaments and artifices, and glass windows had been placed looking out of it on every side; and one of those windows had been fashioned above Bricriu's own cubicle so that from his cubicle he could look out with a clear view over the great house; for he knew that the Ulidians would not permit him to enter the house.

By threats of the use he would make of his bitter tongue if his invitation were refused, Bricriu persuaded the Ulidians and their wives to come to his feast; and though he himself did not enter the house, by speaking separately to his principal guests before each of them entered it, he succeeded in awakening their desire for precedence and for the champion's portion, as he had planned. The episodes which follow, leading up to *Cennach ind Rúanada* have already been briefly referred to above, p. 119.

Cennach in Rúanada itself tells how Cú Roí came in the form of a giant to guarantee that Cú Chulainn would be admitted by all to be the greatest Ulidian warrior in accordance with the judgment already given in the preceding episode of *Fled Bricrenn*. The *cennach* or 'bargain' was that if a warrior were permitted to behead Cú Roí on the night in question, Cú Roí would be permitted to behead that warrior on the night immediately following. On successive nights a Ulidian warrior accepts the challenge. Cú Roí on each occasion picks up his severed head and walks away.

Muinremor, Loíguire Búadach, and Conall Cernach fail to keep the compact, by not appearing on the second night. Cú Chulainn, when his turn comes, gloomily lays his head on the block; the giant strikes him gently with the blunt side of the axe and says: 'Rise up, Cú Chulainn. None of the warriors of Ulster or Ireland can now claim (?) to be equal to thee in valour, or bravery, or truth. The sovranty of the heroes of Ireland is thine from this hour forth, and the Champion's Portion undisputed; and thy wife shall always enter the banqueting-hall before the women of Ulster.'

Cennach ind Rúanada is the oldest known version of the beheading motif, which is of interest to Arthurian scholars by reason of its appearance in several Arthurian tales. The finest of these is the fourteenth-century alliterative English poem known as *Sir Gawayne and the Green Knight*, in which the beheading motif forms the central theme.

The other Ulidian story which tells of wordy argument at a feast corresponds even more closely than *Fled Bricrenn* to the Celtic trait referred to by Posidonius; for in it, as in Posidonius' statement, the warriors actually come to blows as the result of their rivalry. The story is entitled *Scéla Mucce Meic Dá Thó*. It exists in an Old Irish version, dating from c. A.D. 800, and a fourteenth- or fifteenth-century modernization of it. Only the Old Irish version has been published in full.[1] It is a fine specimen of the old abrupt style of story-telling, with some speech-poems interspersed. *Scéla Mucce Meic Dá Thó* is one of the few hero-tales which does not mention Cú Chulainn; in it Conall Cernach takes Cú Chulainn's place as the chief champion of the Ulidians.

The quarrel under consideration took place at a feast prepared by Mac Dá Thó, king of the Leinstermen, for the Ulidians and the men of Connacht. Ailill and Medb, on the one hand, and Conchobar mac Nessa, on the other, had

---

[1] The best edition is that by R. Thurneysen (Dublin, 1935). Mrs. N. K. Chadwick adds an English translation to her edition in her *Early Irish Reader* (1927), pp. 16–24.

asked Mac Dá Thó for a famous hound which he owned. Fearing to offend either party he had promised the hound to both, and by inviting both parties for the same day he hoped that the problem would be solved by the rival parties themselves, without compromising intervention on his own part. The main portion of the feast consisted of a huge pig: 'Sixty milch-cows have been kept feeding it for seven years;[1] but it was out of rancour it used to be fed, in order that the men of Ireland might be slaughtered by reason of it.'

The question was asked how the pig should be divided. Bricriu was present and suggested that it should be divided 'in accordance with battle-victories' (ar chomramaib).

'Let it be so,' said Ailill.

'Good,' said Conchobar: 'we have lads in the house who have travelled over the border.'

'You will have need of your lads to-night, Conchobar,' said Senláech Arad from Crúachain Con Alad in the west: 'often did I cause their buttocks to be wet with the bog-water of Lúachair Dedad; often was one of them left with me like a fat beef.'

'The beef you left with us was fatter,' said Muinremor son of Gerrgenn, 'namely your own brother Crúaichniu son of Rúadlom from Crúachain Con Alad.'

These opening taunts set the tone for similar boasting by other warriors among the guests, whose tauntful thrusts and parries must have delighted early audiences. The taunts of *Scéla Mucce Meic Dá Thó* are worded more roughly and vigorously than the long leisurely taunts which mark the meeting of famous warriors in the *Iliad*.[2] Cet's and Conall's respectful greetings to one another in paragraph 15 of the tale are likewise far more primitive in tone than corresponding courtly exchanges in the *Iliad*.[3] This meeting

---

[1] With the exaggeration contrast the restraint apparent in Greek descriptions of feasts, such as those referred to *supra*, p. 119, n. 2.

[2] The meeting of Achilles and Aeneas, for instance, *Iliad*, XX, 177 sq.

[3] Hector's speech to Aias, for instance, followed by interchange of gifts, after their long duel (*Iliad*, VII, 287 sq.).

of Cet and Conall forms the highlight of the story. It offers a fine example of the sudden magnificent external response to a difficult situation which is a feature of all heroic traditions.

Cet, the chief Connacht champion, had by his taunts successively shamed several Ulidian claimants to the honour of dividing the pig. He had just settled himself to carve it when Conall entered the hall.

The Ulidians joyfully welcomed Conall, and Conchobar removed his hood from his head and waved it.

'I am glad that our food has been prepared', said Conall. 'Who is apportioning it?' 'That has been granted to the man who is doing it,' said Conchobar, 'namely Cet son of Mágu.' 'Is it true, Cet,' said Conall, 'that thou art apportioning the pig?'

Then Cet said:
  Conall is welcome,
  Heart of stone,
  Fierce heat of a lynx,
  Brilliance of ice,
  Red strength of wrath,
  Beneath bosom of a warrior
  Who is wound-dealing and battle-victorious.
  Thou, the son of Findchóem, art comparable to me!

And Conall said:
  Cet is welcome,
  Cet son of Mágu,
  Place where dwells a champion,
  Heart of ice,
  Tail of a swan,
  Strong chariot-warrior in battle,
  Warlike ocean,
  Lovely eager bull,
  Cet son of Mágu!

'Our meeting with one another will make all that clear,' said Conall; 'our parting with one another will make it clear; it will be talked of by drovers and will be attested by cobblers (?);

for roped (?) heroes will march to fierce battle; the two chariot-warriors will wreak slaughter in return for slaughter; man will step over man in this house to-night.'[1]

'But move off from the pig,' said Conall. 'And what would bring thee to it?' said Cet. 'Truly,' said Conall, 'to seek admission of battle-victory for myself: I shall give thee one instance of battle-victory, Cet,' said Conall: 'I swear by that by which my people swear, since I took spear in hand I have never been without slaying a Connachtman every day and plundering by fire every night, and I have never slept without a Connacht-man's head beneath my knee.' 'It is true,' said Cet: 'thou art a better warrior than I. But if it were Ánluan who were here, he would match thee with battle-victory for battle-victory. It is bad for us that he is not in the house.' 'But he is,' said Conall, drawing Ánluan's head from his belt; and he hurled it on to Cet's chest so that blood flowed over his lips.

Then Cet left the pig, and Conall sat down by it.

Conall's hurling at Cet of his brother Ánluan's head is perhaps more barbaric than anything described in the *Iliad*, though Achilles' action in Book XXII, when he dragged Hector's naked corpse behind his chariot, gloating over his victory before the eyes of Hector's aged parents, is essentially as horrifying to civilized minds.

As is so often the case with Irish manuscript versions of an oral tale, the recorder of *Scéla Mucce Meic Dá Thó*, having presented one fine passage more or less as it would have been told to an audience, ends his version with a condensed summary of the succeeding events, which include a battle between the disappointed Connachtmen and the triumphant Ulidians in the house and outer court, the obtaining of the dog by the Ulidians and their use of it to help in the

---

[1] This 'rhetoric', following the lines in archaic alliterative metre, is, like all such rhetorics, hard to understand, and perhaps not in every detail rightly translated. The manner of Cet's address and of Conall's reply is probably based on ancient heroic tradition; for a Tartar chieftain in the last century could show his respect for a distinguished visitor by the utterance of obscure extempore verse (see H. M. and N. K. Chadwick, *The Growth of Literature*, III, 187).

pursuit of the Connachtmen, and the death of the dog, impaled on the shaft of Ailill and Medb's chariot.

That the living tradition of the story was an oral one is suggested not alone by differences between details in the version preserved for us to-day and similar details referred to in two old poems appended by Thurneysen to his edition of the ninth-century tale, but also by the apparent inclusion of the tale, under the title *Argain Meic Dá Thó* (Mac Dá Thó's Slaughter), in the two main lists of tales which *filid* should be able 'to tell to kings and noblemen'.[1]

In a review of Thurneysen's *Irische Helden- und Königsage*, Wolfgang Schultz (ZCP, XIV, 299) claimed that the Irish Heroic tales are essentially mythological and objected to their being treated as distinct from the Mythological tales. More than twenty years later T. F. O'Rahilly in his epoch-making *Early Irish History and Mythology* likewise insisted on the mythological nature of the Heroic tales:

> Actually (he writes, p. 271) the Ulidian tales are wholly mythical in origin, and they have not the faintest connexion with anything that could be called history apart from the fact that traditions of warfare between the Ulaid and the Connachta have been adventitiously introduced into a few of them, and especially into the longest and best-known tale, 'Táin Bó Cualnge.' Cúchulainn, who in the Táin is assigned the role of defender of the Ulaid against their invaders, can be shown to be in origin Lug or Lugaid, a deity whom we may conveniently call the Hero, provided we bear in mind that he was a wholly supernatural personage, and not a mere mortal. The other leading characters, such as Cú Roí, Fergus, Bricriu and Medb, are likewise euhemerized divinities.

Only in nature do we normally find divisions between classes which impose themselves absolutely. In the works of man, on the other hand, classes commonly overlap and distinction between them is largely a matter of convenience. It may well be that Cú Chulainn and Bricriu were originally

[1] See *supra*, pp. 103–4.

divine figures, while Cú Roí still, even in the stories, retains much of his divine nature, and Fergus and Medb, though clearly regarded as human by the story-tellers, can to-day be readily recognized by mythologists as deities whose original divinity had been forgotten.[1] Mythologists there-fore, may well prefer, with Schultz and O'Rahilly, to insist on the mythological aspect of the Heroic cycle. The student of literature, on the other hand, will prefer, with Thurneysen and the Chadwicks, to insist on the realistic human treat-ment of its characters and the general historicity of the back-ground against which they are depicted.

In many of the tales connected with the cycle the historical element may be of very slight importance indeed. These tales are classified with the Heroic cycle merely for reasons of convenience, and may equally well be assigned to other cycles. *Serglige Con Culainn ocus Óenét Emire*, is a case in point. It has already been mentioned above among the Mythological tales. *Tochmarc Emire* (The Wooing of Emer) is another example. It is known to us to-day from a partially lost tenth-century recension, which contains Old Irish strata, and a twelfth-century recension based on it. *Tochmarc Emire* tells how Cú Chulainn, whose three faults were that 'he was too young, too brave, and too beautiful',[2] was tested first by Emer herself in a riddle-contest,[3] and secondly by

[1] The word 'euhemerization' is better reserved for conscious presentation as human beings of characters whom tradition still commonly regarded as divine. The euhemerizing of Núadu and his companions by Irish men of learning, referred to *supra*, p. 105, may thus be distinguished from the for-getting, even in story-lore, of the original divinity of Fergus and Medb.

[2] Cf. Van Hamel's edition, §6 (in his *Compert C. C. and Other Stories*, 1933, p. 22).

[3] The use of riddles to test brides and suitors, as in Cú Chulainn's wooing of Emer, in Finn's wooing of Ailbe, and in a closely connected Donegal folktale, is not confined to Ireland. The Tartars have this theme in many stories (H. M. and N. K. Chadwick, *The Growth of Literature*, III, 153, 158); and in Russia in the last century testing the suitor by riddles was in some districts a living custom (*ib.* II, 211–214). The Wooing of Ailbe and the Donegal folktale will be referred to below in the section entitled The Ossianic Lore and Romantic Tales of Medieval Ireland.

Emer's father, Forgoll Manach (doubtless originally chief god of the Fir Manach tribe, the Irish equivalent of the Gaulish Menapii), by means of an overseas expedition, which in origin was probably an expedition to the other-world. A female warrior called Scáthach, living beyond the Alps, trains Cú Chulainn in warrior feats in the course of this expedition, in which marvellous incidents abound. The atmosphere of marvel which gives its tone to this part of the story enabled it to live on in the post-Norman period when romantic tales were in fashion in Ireland, and the thirteenth-century *Foglaim Con Culainn* (Cú Chulainn's Training) is a modernization of the Scáthach portion of it. *Foglaim Con Culainn* is one of the few Cú Chulainn tales which were still popular with peasant audiences in the eighteenth and nineteenth centuries. In this it resembles the closely con-nected tale of how Cú Chulainn, without knowing it, or only half knowing it, slew Conlaí (later Conláech), the son he had begotten during his stay with Scáthach.[1] Schultz[2] and O'Rahilly[3] believed this to be a native Irish development of an old motif inherited from Indo-European times. In Teutonic lore a similar story is told of Hildebrand and Hadubrand; and Meyer[4] and Thurneysen[5] thought that the theme came to Ireland from a Teutonic source and that it is ultimately traceable to the Persian story of Sohrab and Rustem. That Schultz and O'Rahilly are right is rendered probable by the many survivals in Irish folklore of themes traceable in other Indo-European traditions whose existence in Ireland can hardly be explained by borrowing.[6]

A number of stories, most of them more or less unheroic in tone, yet loosely connected with the Heroic cycle in the

---

[1] The oldest version, belonging perhaps to the ninth or tenth century, is entitled *Aided Áenfir Aífe* (The Death of Aífe's Only Son). That most recently recorded is perhaps the fragment written down from oral tradition about the year 1930 and printed in *Béaloideas*, IX, 57.

[2] ZCP, XIV, 302.   [3] *Early Ir. Hist. and Mythol.*, 62.

[4] *Fianaigecht*, 22.   [5] *Heldensage*, 403.

[6] *Duanaire Finn*, III, xliv, 156, 193–194, 446.

manner of the tales mentioned in the preceding paragraph, used to be grouped by the medieval Irish under the heading *Remscéla* or 'Foretales' to Táin Bó Cúailnge, because they describe episodes which lead up to or explain something about the Táin. Thus *Faillsigud Tána Bó Cúailnge* (The revealing of Táin Bó Cúailnge) explains how the Táin became known to *filid* in the seventh century. It is extant in three short twelfth-century versions, and in a long thirteenth-century version entitled *Tromdám Gúaire* (Gúaire's Burdensome Company). All four versions agree in stating that the Táin was an ancient tale the manuscript of which had been given in exchange for the *Culmen*, or 'Summit (of learning)'. This *Culmen*, to which there are several references in early Irish documents, has been brilliantly identified by T. Ó Máille[1] with the famous *Etymologiae* written in the early seventh century by Isidore of Seville. As a result of the exchange, only fragments of the Táin, it is said, could be, told in Ireland in the seventh century. Ultimately the poet Senchán Torpéist (†657) learnt the whole Táin from the narration of the hero Fergus, who had taken part in it, Fergus having been miraculously restored to life for this purpose.

It has been suggested that this legend is based on a tradition that a version of the Táin was first written down in the seventh century, and Thurneysen in 1932[2] withdrew the objections which he had advanced in his *Heldensage* (p. 111) to so early a date for the recording of Irish lore in writing.

Some of the *Remscéla* such as the charming eighth-century *Aislinge Óenguso* (The Dream of Oengus) are wholly mythological in character, and have very little connection indeed with the Táin. Another of them, the story of Deirdre, the Helen of Ireland, combines in its oldest version a realistic warrior background with a love-theme which may be

---

[1] *Ériu*, IX, 71. See addendum by O'Rahilly, *Ériu*, X, 109.
[2] *Kuhns Zeitschrift für vergl. Sprachforschung*, LIX, 9; ZCP, XIX, 209.

mythological in origin. It explains why Fergus was in exile with Ailill and Medb in Connacht at the time of Táin Bó Cúailnge, and it is one of the finest tales of the Ulidian cycle. The ninth-century version of it, entitled *Longes Mac nUislenn* (The Exile of the Sons of Uisliu), is the earliest version extant of the theme of the elopement of the king's (Conchobar's) destined bride (Deirdre) with one of his warriors (Noísiu son of Uisliu), and the consequent life of the lovers in exile. This theme became a part of the common literary tradition of Europe from its use in the story of Tristan and Isolda, which is traceable ultimately to a Celtic source.[1] Fergus, relying on a promise of Conchobar's, had pledged his word to the three sons of Uisliu that they would not be harmed if they returned to Ulster from their wanderings with Deirdre in Scotland. On their return, however, Conchobar slew them treacherously, and Fergus, having burnt Conchobar's residence at Emain, retired to Ailill and Medb's court at Crúachain in Connacht.

Another of the *Remscéla*, the ninth-century *Táin Bó Froích* (Fróech's Cattle-raid), is a story which is hard to classify. Professor James Carney of the Dublin Institute for Advanced Studies in a public lecture delivered in 1953 in University College, Dublin, has suggested that it is of monastic origin, and is based on a water-monster motif found in saints' lives, and on stories of the countries beyond the Alps brought to Ireland by pilgrims. The first part of *Táin Bó Froích* treats of Fróech's wooing of Ailill's daughter Findabair, and is famous for its description of the beauty of Fróech as he swam in the pool in which he later fought and defeated the water-monster:

> 'Do not come out,' said Ailill, 'till thou bring me a branch from the rowan tree yonder on the bank of the river. Its berries please me.' Fróech went then and broke off a branch from the tree, and brought it back over the water. Findabair used after-

---

[1] An equally early Irish parallel to certain motifs in the Tristan and Isolda story is mentioned *infra*, p. 138, n. 1.

wards to say of any beautiful thing she saw, that she thought it more beautiful to see Fróech coming across a dark pool, the white body, the lovely hair, the shapely face, the grey eye, the gentle youth without fault or blemish, his face narrow below and broad above, his body straight and perfect, the branch with the red berries between his throat and his fair face. Findabair used to say that she had never seen anything half or a third as beautiful as he.[1]

KING TALES

The Chadwicks in their *Growth of Literature* (I, 165) regard the Heroic Age of Ireland as having continued from the pre-historic Ulidian period to the end of the seventh century, the story of *Cath Almaine* (The Battle of Allen), fought in the year 718, and known to us to-day from a ninth-century version, being treated by them as the latest in origin of Irish heroic tales. The Ulidian tales, however, are on the whole the only Irish tales which tend to be truly heroic in spirit. The King cycle, to which *Cath Almaine* belongs, clearly represents a different category of storytelling.

The originators of the Ulidian tradition were interested mainly in heroic character, in loyalty, fidelity to the plighted word, fearlessness in the face of odds and ready external response to a difficult situation. Their best stories treat of some single episode which, while it illustrates heroic character, is often of little historic importance for the community, just as the Greek *Iliad* tells of the wrath of Achilles rather than the history of the war against Troy or the life of the leader of the Myrmidons and the origins of his rule. King tales, on the other hand, show an interest, not primarily in heroic character, but in matters of importance for the community, the origin of peoples or of dynasties, anecdotes about famous representatives of a dynasty, accounts of battles which determined the course of history, or of incidents which

---

[1] Translation by M. E. Byrne and Professor M. Dillon, *Études Celtiques*, II (1937), p. 7, §17.

explain some custom,[1] though much of the heroic outlook, heroic grandeur, heroic savagery, and heroic readiness of response to a difficult situation, is to be found in certain passages of them. They represent primitive history rather than primitive literature, and seldom, therefore, give the modern reader that aesthetic delight which he obtains from the best tales of the Mythological and the true Heroic cycles.

The Heroic Age remembered in Ulidian tradition is what the Chadwicks describe as the princely type of Heroic Age, such as we find in the Greek *Iliad*, the Sanscrit *Mahābhārata*, or the Teutonic Siegfried tales. This type of Heroic Age never lasts for long. The King tales of Ireland are situated in a background more akin to the non-princely type of Heroic Age which the Chadwicks have found existing for long periods in many places, and which it might be better to describe as a turbulent semi-barbarous civilization with heroic tendencies.

The accounts of tribal and dynastic origins inserted in the historical tract known to-day as 'The Laud Genealogies and Tribal Histories' (ZCP, VIII, 291–388) are among the earliest specimens of the King cycle which we possess. Their archaic language suggests that they date from the eighth century. Many of them are mere references or short anecdotes, such as the anecdote which tells how Níall proved to his father Eochu that he was superior to his elder brothers in the prudence which should characterize a king. It was this Níall who established the power of the dynasty which ruled uninterruptedly in Tara from the beginning of the fifth century to the deposition of Máel Shechlainn by Brían Bórama in the year 1002.

Eochu Mugmedón was king of Ireland. Áed asked him which of his sons would be king. 'I do not know,' said he, 'till a smithy

---

[1] Cf. 'That is why it is wrong for any man of the Eóganacht to slay a man of the Crecraige,' at the end of an eighth-century anecdote about the birth of Fíacho Muillethan, ZCP, VIII, 309,22.

be burnt over their heads.' Thereupon a smithy was burnt. Brion, the eldest of the sons, seized the chariot and all its harness. Fíachra seized the wine-vat. Ailill seized all the weapons. Fergus Cáechán seized the pile of dry wood. Níall seized all the smith's implements, including the bellows, the hammers, and the anvil with its block. 'Truly,' said Eochu, 'Níall shall be their king, and his brothers shall serve him.' (ZCP, VIII, 304,31–38).

Others of these early origin legends remind the reader of the usual imperfect manuscript recordings by a man of learning of tales, which often probably, in their living oral forms, whiled away the evening for audiences gathered round the fire of a royal residence on winter nights in the seventh century. Most famous among these is the account (ZCP, VIII, 309–312) of the birth and early life of Cormac mac Airt, semi-mythical ancestor of the dynasty of which Níall was undoubtedly a real representative.

Cormac's father Art is represented in this account as reigning at Tara. He had a Munster ally, Eógan Mór. This Eógan Mór, son of Ailill Mosaulam (king of Munster), was foster-brother, or uterine brother, of Mac Con, a long involved account of whose life precedes the account of the birth and early life of Cormac here under consideration. In the account of Mac Con's life it had been told that he won the kingship of Tara and all Ireland by slaying Art, king of Tara, and Eógan Mór at the battle of Mag Mucruime in Connacht.

The night before that battle Art went with a hundred-and-fifty warriors to the house of Olc Aiche, whose daughter Achtán 'was the most beautiful woman in Ireland'. Achtán's father Olc Aiche used to drink, out of a huge vessel, the milk provided by a hundred cows. Two of Art's men failed to carry the vessel to give a drink to Art; but the girl was able to carry it unaided. She distributed the contents to Art and his men, and was advised that fortune would be propitious if she were to give herself to the king, but she refused to do so without her father's consent.

Olc Aiche comes. 'Where is my drink?' he said. She fills the vessel with milk for him. 'I recognize my little vat,' he said, 'but it is not my milk, the first milk. Where is my drink?' said he: 'this is not it.' The girl tells him. 'What did Art say to thee?' he asked. 'He has said to me: "Fortune would be propitious provided thou wert to go with the king."' 'It would be better for thee to go,' said he. 'I too should like that,' said the girl, 'provided thou didst approve.' 'Good will come of it,' said Olc Aiche, 'provided that thou bear whatever progeny he leaves; and the progeny which thou mayest bear shall be kings of Ireland for ever. Let a feast be prepared for the king by thee, to wit, fifty oxen, fifty boars, five-thousand loaves, and fifty vats full of wine.'[1] All this was brought to Art the next day; and the girl went with them, accompanied by fifty girls; and that food was distributed by Art; and the girl sleeps with him that day, and a tent was made around them, and she repeats her father Olc Aiche's words to him, and she demands a sign for herself, and Art gave her his sword and his gold thumb-ring and his assembly array, and they bid goodbye to one another with great sorrow; and the girl was pregnant with Cormac grandson of Conn.

Shortly after his birth Cormac was carried off from Achtán by a she-wolf, who suckled him with her cubs. A famous trapper called Luigne Fer Trí found him and fed him for a year. Achtán, having discovered this, went to Luigne Fer Trí and explained to him who the child really was. He advised her to hide the child, lest Mac Con should kill it. She therefore took Cormac to the north of Ireland to his father Art's foster-father Fiachna. Fiachna enclosed Cormac in a vessel made of yew covered with a purple cloak, lest he be killed by the hands of the people welcoming him.

When Cormac was thirty years old, assisted by his grandfather's magic, he went to Tara on an auspicious day. There he found a woman weeping.

'Why is the woman weeping?' asked Cormac. 'She is weeping,' said the steward, 'by reason of a judgement passed by the king to her disadvantage, to wit, that her sheep are forfeit for

[1] A difficult sentence has here been left untranslated.

stripping the herbs of the queen's garden.' 'It would be more fitting,' said Cormac, 'that a shearing should be given for a stripping: the man who passed that judgement never passed false judgement before,' said Cormac, 'let me go to him.'

Mac Con realized that the false judgment he had passed indicated that the period destined to him for kingship had come to an end and that Cormac should succeed him. 'He raised his knee up' as a sign of homage, and Cormac began to exercise kingly functions in Tara in his place.

The theme of the rearing of the rightful heir in a distant place, far from his enemy, followed by his recognition and the winning of his inheritance, is widely spread in place and time. It is known to schoolboys in many countries through the legend of Romulus, the founder of Rome, which agrees with the Cormac story in the incident of suckling by a wolf. Herodotus in the fifth century before Christ told it of Cyrus, founder of the Persian empire, in a form which students of Greek mythology recognize as being closely related to the legend of Perseus, the legend of Neleus and Pelias, and the story of the birth of Cypselus, tyrant of Corinth (B.C. 655–625). In Irish tradition it occurs in many forms, the story of the youth of Finn mac Cumaill being the best-known example.

Several later versions of the Mac Con and Cormac incidents referred to above are described or mentioned by Dr. Myles Dillon in his *Cycles of the Kings*, 16–25. The *fili*-tale, *Cath Maige Mucruime* (Battle of Mag Mucruime), mentioned in both the long-tale-lists referred to *supra*, p. 103, would doubtless, as told orally in the ninth and succeeding centuries, have narrated some or all of these incidents less summarily and without the incoherences which mar them in the extant versions.

Stories about Cormac often impress the reader as being stories in the true sense of the word, told to delight rather than to instruct. In one of them, the twelfth-century *Echtra Chormaic i dTír Tairngire*, 'Cormac's Journey to the Land of Promise' (extant also in an Early Modern version entitled *Faghâil Chraoibhe Cormaic mhic Airt*, 'The Finding of Cormac son of Art's Branch'), he visits the otherworld, a journey to which by his uncle Conlae, on the invitation of a fairy lover, is recorded in the eighth-century *Echtrae Chonlai Choím maic Cuind Chétchathaig* (The Journey of Conlae the Fair son of Cond of the Hundred Battles). Conlae, unlike Cormac, never returned. In another, the tenth-century *Esnada Tige Buichet* or 'Sounds of Buichet's House' (extant also in an eleventh-century verse recension), there is a charming account of how Cormac, having seen his future wife Eithne engaged in the menial tasks of milking cows, drawing water, and cutting rushes, fell in love with her. O'Rahilly in an interesting article on Buchet the Herdsman (*Ériu*, XVI, 7–20) discusses the mythological origin of *Esnada Tige Buichet*, and Dr. Myles Dillon in his *Early Irish Literature* (p. 83) compares the Irish story to the 'Indian legend of Sakuntalā made famous by Kalidāsa'.

As other specimens of origin tales in the King cycle we may mention: the origin tale of the Leinster dynasty, entitled *Orguin Denna Ríg* (The Destruction of Dinn Ríg), extant in an imperfectly narrated ninth-century version; the origin tale of the Ulster sept known as Dál mBúain, which, in its eleventh-century form,[1] tells of the tragic love of Baile Binnbérlach mac Búain (Baile of the Musical Speech son of Búan) for Aillenn of Leinster; stories concerning Conall Corc, reputed founder of Cashel, the chief stronghold of Munster, of which the eighth or ninth-century *Longes Chonaill Chuirc* (Exile of Conall Corc) is an example; the origin tale of the Munster Eóganacht families narrated summarily in eighth-century Irish in the Laud tract already mentioned,[2] and incorporated in another form in *Cath Maige Léna* (The Battle of Mag Léna), a well-told Early Modern King tale, composed probably by a Munster poet for some

---

[1] Edited by E. O'Curry, *Manuscript Materials* (1878), 472 sq.
[2] *Supra*, p. 132. Cf. Meyer's edition, ZCP, VIII, 312–313.

O'Sullivan chieftain in the thirteenth century; the long early-twelfth-century semi-historical compilation which tells of the origin of the Bórama tribute claimed from the Leinstermen by the kings of Tara, and of various efforts to exact it. The Bórama compilation includes the tragic tale of Fithir and Dáirine which, from the story point of view, is better told as an episode in the late-twelfth-century *Acallam na Senórach* or 'Colloquy of the Ancient Men' which will be described at some length below in the section on The Ossianic Lore and Romantic Tales of Medieval Ireland. One of the poets' tale-lists includes *Tochmarc Fithirne ocus Dáirine, dá Ingen Túathail* (The Wooing of Fithirne and Dáirine, the two Daughters of Túathal) as a separate tale. In the form in which we have it, as an episode in longer compilations, it tells how the king of Leinster won for his wife the elder daughter of Túathal, king of Tara.[1] The king of Leinster did not love her. Having therefore confined her to a dwelling in the forest, he wooed the younger daughter. The sisters met, and one died of shame and the other of grief for her. Warfare resulted, till finally, according to the Bórama tract, the Leinstermen agreed to pay a large *éraic* or fine, which was the origin of the tribute known as the Bórama.

Exigencies of space forbid mention of many other tales of the King cycle. One group of them, however, occupies so important a place that it deserves brief treatment here. The group in question consists of traditions about seventh-century or early-eighth-century events. A fine early example is the tragic *Fingal Rónáin* or 'Slaying by Rónán of One of his own Kin', extant in an imperfectly preserved but clearly once well-told tenth-century version. *Fingal Rónáin* narrates the tragic slaying by Rónán king of Leinster (†624) of his beloved son Máel Fothartaig, who had been falsely accused by his stepmother of trying to ravish her.[2] Anecdotes

---

[1] The versions do not agree as to which was the elder, Dáirine or Fithir.

[2] Máel Fothartaig is therefore the Irish equivalent of the Greek Hippolytus, against whom his stepmother Phaedra made a similar accusation.

and tales connected with the east-Ulster king, Mongán mac Fíachnai (†625), or with the Connacht Gúaire (†662), famous for his generosity, afford other examples of this class of tale. Still another example is the story of the Hebridean Cano son of Gartnán (†688), one aspect of which has been already discussed on pp. 99–101.[1] Several tales connected with the battle of Mag Rath, fought in 637, afford further examples of the group of stories under consideration: the most famous of them is the twelfth-century *Buile Suibne* or 'Madness of Suibne', which tells how Suibne, an east-Ulster king, through the curse of a saint went mad from terror in the battle and lived in the wilderness among birds and wild animals; it contains some of the finest nature poetry in Irish literature. The latest in origin of these seventh and early-eighth-century stories are those concerning Cathal mac Finguine (†742) and his contemporaries or close predecessors: they include *Mór Muman ocus Aided Cúanach maic Cailchéni*, 'Mór of Munster and the Death of Cúanu son of Cailchéne' (extant in a ninth-century version); the amusing *Aislinge Meic Con Glinne*, or 'Vision seen by Mac Con Glinne' (extant in two twelfth-century versions), in which Cathal is pictured as afflicted by a demon of gluttony; and the tale of the Battle of Allen already referred to on p. 131.

Though tales either definitely belonging to the King cycle, such as *Serc Gormlaithe do Níall Glúndub* (Gormlaith's Love for Níall Glúndub, slain by the Norse of Dublin in 917),[2] or at least closely related to that cycle, came into existence sporadically in later times when circumstances resembling

---

[1] The story of Cano is of special interest to scholars for the close parallel it contains to certain motifs in the Tristan and Isolda story. This parallel has been discussed by Dr. Myles Dillon in his *Cycles of the Kings*, 79–80. Cf. also *supra*, p. 130, n. 1.

[2] We know the plot of this story, the title of which is given in both of the two main tale-lists, from various references in annals. Moving poems connected with it, clearly from an Early Modern version of the story, are the only traces of a text of it which survive to-day.

those of the ancient King period favoured their growth,[1] it may be said with truth that the originating of King tales came to an end in the course of the first half of the eighth century. This cessation of legend-origination about kings may be partly connected with the more orderly behaviour of the kings themselves; for even to-day stories tend to be narrated of those who are rebels against reason rather than of those who follow the ways of law. It is doubtless, however, to a still greater extent due to the growth of a more critically rational outlook on the part of the recorders of kingly tradition, whose function it was to preserve memory of the past for succeeding generations: annal-making and the tendency to rely on written documents had brought legend-origination to an end among the recorders of kingly tradition.

Of all the King tales *Togail Bruidne Dá Derga* (The Destruction of Dá Derga's Hostel) is the finest. The best-known version of it is that narrated mainly in ninth-century Irish and preserved to-day in the early-twelfth-century *Lebor na hUidre* and other manuscripts. This version, as Thurneysen has shown (*Heldensage*, 623 sq.), is apparently due to an eleventh-century redactor who compiled it, not over-skilfully, from two ninth-century texts known to him. It tells of the slaying of Conaire the Great (son of Etarscél), king of Tara at some ancient period before the rise to power of the dynasty to which the Níall already mentioned on p. 132 belonged. Conaire is represented as a model king, who was induced by the hidden influence of the *áes síde* to violate his *gesa*

---

[1] The dramatic rise to power, at the end of the tenth and beginning of the eleventh century, of Brían Bórama, ancestor of the O'Briens, and his victories over the Norse, gave rise to literary compositions and folktales which have been admirably discussed by Dr. A. J. Goedheer in his *Irish and Norse Traditions about the Battle of Clontarf*, Haarlem, 1938 (the folktales are mentioned on p. 71). Some traditions from the Norse period of Irish history, and some later traditions, such as those of the rise to power of the O'Donnells, Maguires, and MacSweeneys, have been briefly discussed by G. Murphy, *Glimpses of Gaelic Ireland* (1948), 35–43.

(religious prohibitions, or taboos), thus bringing upon himself an inevitable doom. This tale is Greek rather than Irish in its mounting sense of impending tragedy, as its hearers, and ultimately Conaire himself, realize that the *gesa* are being violated one by one, some unconsciously, others consciously but against Conaire's will. And, greatest tragedy of all, those who play one of the most important parts in slaying Conaire are his own foster-brothers, bound to betray him by reason of a general oath sworn to a British pirate, with no thought of the particular application in which it might result.

Togail Bruidne Dá Derga is linked to the Ulidian cycle both by its heroic spirit and by the presence in it of some of the warriors who normally appear only in that cycle. Conall Cernach, for instance, normally appears only in Ulidian tales, but he is depicted as having been with Conaire when Dá Derga's hostel, in which Conaire had taken refuge, was destroyed. This is the account, typical of the heroic spirit, of how his father Amairgin received Conall when he arrived home from the battlefield on which his lord had been slain:

Conall Cernach escaped from the hostel; and one-hundred-and-fifty spears had pierced the arm on which he had his shield. He travelled till he reached his father's house, with half his shield on his arm, and his sword and the fragments of his two spears in his hand. He found his father before the enclosure surrounding his stronghold in Teltown.

'Swift are the wolves that have hunted thee, lad,' said his father.

'Our wounds have come from a conflict with fighting men, old warrior,' said Conall Cernach.

'Thou hast news of Dá Derga's hostel,' said Amairgin. 'Is thy lord alive?'

'He is not alive,' said Conall.

'I swear by the gods by whom the great tribes of the Ulidians swear, it is cowardly for the man who has escaped alive, having left his lord with his foes in death,' said Conall Cernach's father.

'My wounds are not white, old warrior,' said Conall. He showed him his shield arm. One-hundred-and-fifty wounds had been inflicted on it; but the shield which protected it had saved it. As for the right arm, it had been twice as badly used; for, though the sinews of that arm held to the body without being parted, it had been hacked, cut, wounded, and riddled, since there was no shield guarding it.

'That arm fought this night, lad,' said Amairgin.

''Tis true, old warrior,' said Conall Cernach: 'many are they to whom it gave drinks of death this night in front of the hostel.'

Togail Bruidne Dá Derga is a tale which it is hard to classify. Conaire would seem to have belonged to the people known as Érainn, who in historical times were confined to Co. Cork in south Munster, but had once been widely spread over Ireland; there is reason to believe that the Ulidians themselves were closely related to them. T. F. O'Rahilly has shown[1] that, according to various sources, Laginians (in historical times the men of Leinster), as well as British pirates, were responsible for Conaire's death. He holds with probability that the tale of his death in a burning hostel, and of the apparent burning of the homesteads of Meath by the *áes síde* which led to it, may (apart from mythological elements) ultimately be traced to vague memories of the first night of the Laginian invasion of Ireland from Britain, in the third century before Christ, told from the point of view of the Érainn who ruled in Tara at the period.[2] O'Rahilly also[3] gives good reason for believing that the story of the Destruction of Dinn Ríg, already mentioned on p. 136, represents a tradition of the Laginian invasion told from the Laginian point of view. 'We are fortunate,' he writes (*l.c.* 140), 'in possessing a double account of this

---

[1] *Early Irish History and Mythology*, 119–120.

[2] The Ulidian tale known as *Togail Bruidne Dá Choca*, 'The Destruction of Dá Choca's Hostel' (extant to-day only in a thirteenth or fourteenth-century version, and discussed by O'Rahilly, *l.c.* 130–140) clearly represents a different tradition of what is essentially the same story.

[3] *l.c.* 103–117.

invasion, one of them told from the viewpoint of the invaded, the other from that of the invader, so that we are enabled the more easily to realize the tragedy on the one side, the triumph on the other.'

LATER DEVELOPMENT

In the course of the twelfth century Irish literature was enriched by several versions of classical stories, such as *Togail Troí* (The Destruction of Troy), an Irish adaptation of the *De Excidio Troiae* attributed to Dares Phrygius, and *Imthechta Áeníasa* (The Wanderings of Aeneas), based on Virgil's *Aeneid*. The Latin texts were freely altered, however, to suit Irish taste. Some of Virgil's most beautiful passages, the metaphor, for instance (*Aeneid*, XII, 473–478), by which Iuturna is likened to a swallow flying through the halls of a rich man's house in search of food for her young, are omitted by the adaptor, while elsewhere he inserts descriptive passages modelled on Irish saga tradition. It is doubtful however, whether these classical adaptations ever entered into the living tradition of storytelling in Ireland.

Storytelling in the Heroic and Kingly traditions seems, with some exceptions, to have lost its vitality in the changed Ireland which resulted from the Anglo-Norman invasion of 1175, partly, it is probable, because that invasion put an end to the kingly *óenaige* already mentioned on p. 103, where the *fili* would have above all found hearers who would have both expected and appreciated it. The Finn tales and Romantic tales, which became the principal tales in the petty lordships which characterized medieval Ireland, after kingly Ireland had ceased to exist, will be dealt with in the next section under the title The Ossianic Lore and Romantic Tales of Medieval Ireland.

III

THE OSSIANIC LORE AND ROMANTIC TALES OF MEDIEVAL IRELAND

IN Saga and Myth in Ancient Ireland, the preceding section in this book, tales of gods, heroes, and kings have been
described. When those aristocractically-conditioned tales were
being told in king's palaces and at royal *óenaige*[1] in ninth- and
tenth-century Ireland, simple folk, seated by their firesides
or in their fishing-boats, probably preferred to tell magically-
controlled tales about Fionn mac Cumhall and his Fiana,
such as their descendants have continued to tell down to
the present day. For not alone are the earliest scraps of
learned legend about Fionn akin in spirit to the simple tales
of magic marvel told about him by folkstory-tellers to-day,
but references to the interest taken in Fionn and his companions by *daoscarshluagh* and *criadhaireadha* ('common
folk' and 'peasants') are traceable in the literature from the
eleventh century on. With the passage of time, however,
even learned storytellers decided to weave new artistic tales
about Fionn and his Fiana, and beginning about the early
twelfth century a succession of poets formed a ballad
literature concerning them, so that when we come to the
sixteenth century Fionn is a more prominent figure in every
stratum of Gaelic narrative lore than Lugh, Cú Chulainn,
Conaire, and those other gods, heroes, and kings, to whom
the highest rank in the hierarchy of storytelling had in early
times been awarded.

Cú Chulainn's fame has until recently been confined to
Ireland. The names of Fionn, however (under the altered
form Fingal), of his son Ossian (in Irish Oisín), and of his
grandson Oscar, had by the nineteenth century become
household words wherever the romantic literary movement
had taken root. For this we have to thank the Scottish James

[1] Modern Irish *aonaighe*, 'fairs'.

145

Macpherson, who, in 1762 and 1763, published his *Fingal* and *Temora*, supposed to have been translated from epic poems written by 'Ossian' in the third or fourth century of our era. James Macpherson's epics were mainly a figment of his own imagination, but the names of their heroes, and some of the incidents described, were based on genuine Gaelic balladry about Fionn, Oisín, Oscar and the other Fiana. Men such as Napoleon in France and Goethe in Germany loved to read Macpherson's work, which was translated into many European languages and helped to awaken that interest in Celtic studies which has resulted not alone in the disproval of Macpherson's claim to be nothing more than a translator, but also in the better knowledge which men of learning all over Europe to-day have concerning Irish literature and the true nature of 'Ossianic' balladry.

Most of the ballads about Fionn Mac Cumhall and his Fiana are attributed by the ballad-makers to Fionn's son Oisín. Scottish Gaelic forms of Oisín's name (such as Oisean) gave rise to Macpherson's Ossian, from which the adjective Ossianic has been formed to describe the cycle as a whole, and in particular the ballad portion of it. The warbands ruled by Fionn have always been known as *fiana*, originally a common noun meaning bands of professional warriors, but in later usage confined to Fionn's Fiana. These Fiana have provided the Irish name for the cycle, *Fianaigheacht*, or lore about the Fiana (often to-day anglicized as Fenian lore). The ballad portion of the cycle is usually described in Irish as *Laoithe Fianaigheachta*, Fenian Lays (or ballads), though the term *Laoithe Oisín* (Oisin's Lays) is common in modern manuscripts.

Who was this Fionn mac Cumhaill (literally 'Fair One, son of Cumhall'[1]), who was destined to attain so important a place in Irish narrative tradition?

---

[1] In certain ancient references the father's name is given as Umall (not Cumall), and Umall may be the original form. The oldest spelling of Fionn's

In the seventh, eight and following centuries, Irish men of learning constructed a history of Ireland on the model of biblical history and the history of Greece and Rome. Having little to guide them except stories, and a number of genealogies which traced the origin of important families to pagan gods, they altered these traditions, producing what John MacNeill used to call 'Irish synthetic history', an account of Irish origins going back to the time of Adam. In this synthetic history a place was ultimately found for Fionn, and, at least from the eleventh century, Irish men of learning were unanimous in holding that Fionn mac Cumhaill was captain of King Cormac's professional soldiery in the early third century of the Christian era. To-day, however, students of Irish origins, distrusting the artificial construction of the synthetic historians, prefer to draw their own conclusions from what remains of the traditions upon which they worked.

The oldest stories about Fionn, and modern folklore, two sources which have on the whole been little influenced by the doctrine of the synthetic historians, point definitely to Fionn's having been originally a mythological figure possessing some kinship with the god Lugh (cf. *infra*, p. 161). Lugh ('The Bright One') was the fighter of battles with otherworld beings and had for his chief opponent the one-eyed Balar, whose eye used to burn up whatever it looked on directly. Fionn ('The Fair One') likewise is the fighter of battles with otherworld beings and has for his chief opponent Aodh, who was nicknamed Goll: Aodh means 'fire', and Goll means 'one-eyed'. Several Gaulish places have been named after Lugh, among them Lyons (Lugudunum) and Laon (Lugudunum Remorum). In primitive Celtic, Fionn's name would have appeared as Uindos, which seems to have had a byform Uindonos;[1] Celtic placenames such as

[1] *Dunaire Finn*, III, p. lxxxii.

own name is Find. As the cycle under consideration was specially popular in Ireland in modern times, modern Irish spellings will be used here unless some particular reason calls for use of older forms.

Uindobona (Austrian Vienna) and several Uindonissas (among them Swiss Windisch in the canton of Aargau and French Vendresse in the Ardennes) seem therefore to show Fionn giving his name to Celtic places just as the divine Lugh did. Moreover Lugh appears in Welsh tradition as the magic Lleu, and Fionn, the magic warrior-hunter of Ireland, seems to appear there also as the magic warrior-hunter Gwyn ab Nudd, whose name, using a reconstruction in primitive Celtic of the Welsh forms, might be translated Uindos son of Nodons; but though Welsh and Irish traditions often agree in mythology, they hardly ever do so where history is concerned. The combined force of these and other arguments[1] leaves, therefore, little room for doubt but that Fionn originally belonged to the realm of mythology rather than of history.

EARLY FIONN TALES

A summary account of the earliest references to Fionn in Irish documents will be found in *Duanaire Finn*, Part III, p. lv sq. As an example of them we may cite the legend of Fionn and Cúldubh, of which a version in eighth- or ninth-century Irish has been edited by Meyer (RC, XXV, 344–347):

> When the Fian were at Badamair on the brink of the Suir, Cúldub of the race of Birgge came out of Síd ar Femun[2] *ut Scotti dicunt* and carried off their cooking from them. For three nights he acted thus towards them. The third time, however, *norat* Finn and he went ahead to Síd ar Femun. Finn thrust successfully at him as he entered the *síd* and he fell on the far side. While he was drawing his hand towards him he was interfered

---

[1] Set out at length in *Duanaire Finn*, III, and more summarily by T. F. O'Rahilly in his *Early Irish History and Mythology*.

[2] Síd ar Femun (The Fairy Hill before Femen, or, if we read the older *al* for *ar*, the Fairy Hill beyond Femen) is to-day known as Slievenamon, north of Clonmel, Co. Tipperary.

with by a woman from the *síd* with a dripping vessel in her hand from which she had just been distributing drink, and she jammed the door against the *síd*, and Finn squeezed his finger between the door and the post. When the finger came out again he began to utter an incantation; mystic knowledge illuminated him and he said:

> Come to Femen. A judgement!
> A happy blow from a long ever-swift shaft
> Increases my dish by a pig;
> It is Finn's ale-drinking at Cúldub's tomb we chant.

This paragraph on Fionn and Cúldubh is clearly not a story in the literary sense. Indeed the use of Latin words such as *norat*, 'knew', in the Old Irish narrative already sufficiently indicates its learned affinities. It occurs in a law-text as an illustration of the type of incantation known as *imbas forosnai*, 'mystic knowledge which illuminates', in most examples of which the last words of the incantation reveal the knowledge which is being sought, here probably originally the name of the mysterious stealer of the Fian's cooked pig; for another Old Irish version of the anecdote[1] makes it clear that the meal the Fian were cooking consisted of a pig. By representing Fionn's opponents as *aos sídhe* (Otherworld Folk) rather than human beings the paragraph quoted is in agreement with all other Old Irish tradition about Fionn and most modern folklore; and from consideration of various other sources we can be certain that it is essentially a learned man's summary account of one of the most fundamental Fionn traditions, that which tells how he slew his chief otherworld opponent Aodh (here called Cúldubh, 'The Black-haired One') with a specially provided spear. Accounts of how[2] Fionn slew this chief opponent commonly introduce an explanation of his peculiar gift of

[1] Meyer in RC, XIV (1893), 245 sq., R. D. Scott, *The Thumb of Knowledge* (1930), 8 sq.; Dr. Hull in *Speculum*, XVI (1941), 329 sq.
[2] T. F. O'Rahilly, *Early Irish History and Mythology*, 328 sq.; *Duanaire Finn*, III, lxiv sq., lxx, lxxii sq.

divining by chewing his thumb. The squeezing of the finger in the door of the otherworld dwelling here corresponds to that explanation, which ultimately definitely takes the form of Fionn's burning his thumb to smooth a blister on a magic salmon he was cooking.

The evidence of this and similar early references to Fionn goes to show that in the eight, ninth and tenth centuries, when tales of the Mythological, Heroic, and King cycles were flourishing, Fionn, though well known to men of learning, was confined in their learned lore to short anecdotes connecting him with fighting, hunting, wooing, and other-world incidents all over Ireland. Certain tenth-century references suggest that the tendency to associate him specially with Cormac king of Tara was then becoming general, and from the eleventh century on, as has already been pointed out (p. 147), it was the accepted doctrine of the schools that Fionn had been captain of Cormac's professional soldiery.

We have already had occasion to mention above (p. 103) two long lists of tales which a twelfth-century *fili* should have been able to tell. One of those lists has only two titles of Fionn tales. The other, that contained in the Book of Leinster transcribed about the year 1160, repeats those two titles and, in addition, gives three others. The titles both lists give are *Tochmarc Ailbe* (The Wooing of Ailbhe) and *Aithed Gráinne re Diarmait* (The Elopement of Gráinne with Diarmaid); and Thurneysen, it is to be noted, holds that, where both lists agree, the tales about which they agree were regarded as *fili*-tales already in the tenth century. Of the three extra titles contained in the Book of Leinster list, one, *Uath Beinne Étair* (The Cave of Howth), seems to be extant to-day as a thirteenth- or fourteenth-century anecdote[1] in archaised language of an incident which could have occurred during the Elopement of Gráinne with Diarmaid; the second, *Echtra Finn i nDerc Ferna* (Fionn's Journey into the

---

[1] Ed. by Meyer, RC, XI, 129 sq.

Cave of Dunmore, Co. Kilkenny) is to-day unknown; and the third, *Uath Dercce Ferna* (The Cave of Dunmore), was doubtless an episode from it.

The fewness of the refe. nces to Fionn tales in these twelfth-century lists indicates that in the first half of that century Fianaigheacht was only beginning to be regarded as an important branch of Irish story-telling.

Tochmarc Ailbe, the earliest elaborate tale concerning Fionn which we possess to-day is preserved complete in only one sixteenth-century manuscript, though the riddle portion is to be found in two other manuscripts as well. Corruptions in the text make it hard to be certain about its date; but the poems, 'rhetorics', and riddles, which form an important part of it, are at least as early as the tenth century, and probably earlier. The tale tells how Fionn, in his old age, wooed and won Cormac's youngest daughter Ailbhe, testing her suitability to be his wife by means of riddles, and enticing her to share his forest home by describing its birds, animals, fish, fruit, and other woodland amenities. Love of the chase and of the natural riches of the earth are a regular theme in the Fionn cycle at all periods. The theme of testing a bride or suitor by means of riddles is an international one, which has already been discussed in treating of Cú Chulainn's Wooing of Eimhear.'[1] In a Donegal folktale, recorded early in the present century by Henry Morris,[2] a daughter of Cormac's called Eachnais is won by the son of the King of Connacht, in disguise, as the result of his skill in various riddling conversations which he carried on with her. Eachnais is doubtless a folk corruption of the older name Ailbhe, both consisting of two syllables with the only clear vowel a stressed *a* in the first of the two syllables.

In paragraph 1 of the extant version of *Tochmarc Ailbe*

---

[1] See above, p. 127.
[2] In *Maighdean an tSoluis agus Sgéalta eile*; *sgéalaidhthe Thíre Conaill d'innis*; *Feargus mac Róigh* [i.e. Henry Morris] *a sgríobh síos agus a chuir i n-eagar* (1913), 38–44.

Fionn is depicted as being at enmity with Cormac: 'The cause of the quarrel,' we are told, 'was that Gráinne had given her hatred to Fionn and had given love to Diarmaid ua Duibhne.'

Tochmarc Ailbe therefore supposes knowledge of the story of Diarmaid and Gráinne, which is mentioned in both tale-lists under the title *Aithed Gráinne re Diarmait* (The Elopement of Gráinne with Diarmaid).[1] No early version of this story has been preserved, but the Middle Irish commentary on *Amra Choluim Chille* (The Glories of Colum Cille) cites a ninth- or tenth-century stanza supposed to have been spoken by 'Gráinne daughter of Cormac to Fionn,' which doubtless originally formed part of it:

> There is one
> On whom I should gladly gaze,
> For whom I would give the bright world,
> All of it, all of it, though it be an unequal bargain.[2]

References such as this to incidents in the story enable us to be certain that its framework (the elopement, the lovers' life in the wilderness, and the killing of Diarmaid by a magic boar as the result of treachery on the part of Fionn) is ancient, while the fact that dolmens all over Ireland are known as 'the bed of Diarmaid and Gráinne', and that many landmarks are connected with the lovers, proves its popularity.[3] The only complete telling of the tale which has been preserved can hardly, however, be older than the fourteenth century, and may indeed not be much older than the earliest extant text of it, that in the Royal Irish Academy manuscript, 24 P 9, transcribed by David Ó Duibhgeannáin in 1651. This Early Modern telling of the story is entitled

---

[1] A tenth- or eleventh-century account of how Caoilte collected 'a couple of every wild animal in Ireland' as a bridal gift from Fionn to Gráinne likewise supposes knowledge of Fionn's betrothal to Gráinne (cf. *Duanaire Finn*, III, p. 19).

[2] *Lebor na hUidre*, ed. by R. I. Best and Osborn Bergin, 514–517.

[3] Cf. *Duanaire Finn*, III, xxxvi.

Tóraigheacht Diarmada agus Ghráinne, 'The Pursuit of Diarmaid and Gráinne'. Dr. Myles Dillon has given a good summary of the *Tóraigheacht* in his *Early Irish Literature* (1948), 42–48.

It is clear (he writes) that the story of Gráinne is a variant of the story of Deirdre, the tragedy of a young girl betrothed to an old man and of the conflict between passion and duty on the part of her lover. In both cases death is the price of love. It has been shown by Gertrude Schoepperle that these two stories represent the Celtic source of the story of Tristan and Isolt, and that 'The Pursuit of Diarmaid and Gráinne' preserves a number of motifs which recur in French and German versions of the great romance.

In a footnote Dr. Dillon points out that the Irish saga of Cano son of Gartnán[1] presents another parallel: 'Here, he writes, 'even the name of the old king, Marcán, coincides with French tradition.'

Ossianic balladry will be discussed later in this section. Several of the ballads treat of some moment in the story of Diarmaid and Gráinne. One in particular, a twelfth-century poem put in the mouth of Gráinne as she watches over the sleeping Diarmaid, has been universally admired. In it the following verses are to be found:

> May your sleep be like that slept in the south by good Fiodhach of the noble poets, when he carried off long-lived Morann's daughter in spite of Conall from the Craobhruadh.

> May it be like the sleep in the north of fair comely Fionnchadh of Assaroe, when, by a well-laid plan, he carried off Sláine in spite of Hard-headed Fáilbhe.

> May it be like the sleep in the west of Áine daughter of Gáilian, when she fared once by torchlight with Dubhthach from Dairinis.

> May it be like the sleep in the east of proud daring Deadhaidh, when he carried off Coincheann daughter of Beann in spite of Deicheall of the Dark Weapons.

[1] See above, p. 138, n. 1.

153

Commenting on those verses in her *Tristan and Isolt*, Gertrude Schoepperle has written (p. 392):

> *Nous avons perdu le monde et le monde nous*, says Isolt to Tristan. The solitude of their forest life is peopled for the French poets by no tales of other lovers who have felt and lived as they. But the Celtic Gráinne sings her lover to sleep in the forest with stories of many another that has shared their fate.

Indeed the frequency of the elopement theme in Irish tradition is among the chief arguments which convince scholars of the Celtic origin of the Tristan legend. It is to be noted too that the effort to make Tristan blameless by means of the accidental drinking of a love-potion occurs in a more primitive form in Irish tradition, where both Naoise and Diarmaid act under the binding effect of what in Modern Irish are known as *geasa*. Whatever, in pagan days, may have been the rules governing the imposition of such binding injunctions, in later Irish story-tradition they are imposed freely, often leading to a tragic conflict of duties. As Deirdre bound Naoise to elope with her, so did Gráinne bind Diarmaid; and modern folk-tradition renders even Gráinne blameless by insisting that Diarmaid had a 'love-spot' which compelled Gráinne to love him when she accidentally saw it.

EARLY FIONN BALLADS AND ACALLAM NA SENÓRACH

Up to the twelfth century, as we have seen, Fionn, though clearly well known in Irish tradition, had held no important place in the narrative lore of the *filidh*. By the end of that century, however, Fionn and his Fiana had advanced well on their way towards that pre-eminent position which was ultimately to be theirs.

The twelfth was indeed a century of progress in many departments of Irish life. In the course of it a vigorous reform movement was proceeding in the ecclesiastical sphere, which by the middle of the century had resulted in a change from abbatial to episcopal rule of dioceses and in the territorial delimitation of them. Where civil government was concerned High Kings were beginning to exercise authority in the domains of local kings after the manner of national monarchs. In the artistic sphere we may note the building of several fine churches in the new Hiberno-Romanesque style; while where literature is concerned the great monastic manuscripts were being compiled on which our knowledge of Old and Middle Irish literature is largely based; these manuscripts are *Lebor na hUidre* (The Book of the Dun Cow) compiled in the opening years of the century; its companion Clonmacnois codex,[1] compiled in the first quarter of the century, which, along with much native matter, contains the biblical poem known as *Saltair na Rann* (The Psalter of Quatrains); and the *Lebor Laignech* (Book of Leinster) compiled in the third quarter of the century. Some years before the century began, the *Liber Hymnorum* had been compiled to preserve memory of the hymnology of the ancient Irish church; and in the course of the century several recensions were made of *Lebor Gabála Érenn* (The Book of the Conquest of Ireland) and of *Dinnshenchus Érenn* (The Place-lore of Ireland) to give final form, as it were, to the work of the synthetic historians. The twelfth century was also a century of great story-making activity. *Táin Bó Cuailnge* was rewritten in what is known as the Book of Leinster version at the beginning of the century, and the re-writer of the *Táin* wrote also what Thurneysen[2] regarded as a wholly new addition to the Heroic cycle, under the title *Cath Ruis na Ríg* (The Battle of Rosnaree). Also in the course of the twelfth century *Togail Troí* (The Destruction of Troy), *Togail Tebe* (The Destruction of Thebes), *Merugud Ulix* (The Wandering of Ulysses), *Imthechta Áeníasa* (The Wanderings of Aeneas), and *In*

---

[1] Rawlinson B. 502, preserved in the Bodleian library, Oxford.
[2] See his *Irische Helden- und Königsage* (1921), 364.

Cath Catharda (The Civil War of the Romans), were adapted from Latin for the Irish story-loving public.

The Fionn cycle also benefited from this tendency to add to the recording of ancient tradition, and under the title *Macgnímartha Finn* (Fionn's Boyhood Deeds) some twelfth-century man of learning put together a poorly constructed but valuable account of how Fionn was reared as a posthumous child in the forest and, having won his name of Fionn (The Fair One), slew his opponent Aodh (Fire) with a specially provided spear.[1] Various references in poems of the twelfth and following centuries, and in the pseudo-historical twelfth-century Fionn-tale *Fotha Catha Cnucha* (The Cause of the Battle of Castleknock), prove that this story of Fionn's youth was always well known orally in various versions. During the past hundred years it has likewise been a favourite in different forms with unlettered storytellers all over Ireland and Scotland. These excellent folk-versions can hardly derive from the poorly constructed twelfth-century recording of the story, extant to-day in a single manuscript only. It therefore seems certain that the tale has at all times been essentially a folktale. To Arthurian scholars it has a particular interest as affording a close Celtic parallel to the boyhood story of Perceval as narrated by the late-twelfth-century Chrétien de Troyes in his *Perceval le Gallois* (alternatively known as *Le Cont de Graal*).[2]

The twelfth-century texts which have been referred to in the preceding paragraphs would all have been regarded by their authors as either the recording or the improvement of ancient tradition, and the mode of treatment accorded them was therefore controlled by tradition. Where Fionn, however, was concerned a clearly defined learned story-tradition can hardly be said to have existed at the beginning of the twelfth century, as there were then only a very few *fili*-tales connected with him. Nevertheless he was a figure known to every Irishman by reason of the many magically-controlled

[1] Cf. *supra*, pp. 147, 149.   [2] For other parallels see p. 135.

folktales told about him; moreover the synthetic historians had found a definite place for him in their historical scheme. His cycle was thus eminently suited for further development at the hands of learned storytellers in accordance with the progressive spirit of the century. It is hardly surprising, therefore, to find that in addition to the attention paid by the learned to the folktales about Fionn's youth, the Fionn-cycle was in the course of the twelfth century enriched by many lyrics and by the new genre of balladry, which about this time makes its first appearance in Ireland. This embellishment of the Fionn cycle culminated in the last quarter of the century in the composing of *Acallam na Senórach* (The Colloquy of the Ancient Men), which is perhaps the most pleasing of the many pleasing products of Middle-Irish inventive genius.

In his great work on *European Balladry* (1939) (pp. 16–17), William J. Enthwistle has given as the most satisfactory definition of a ballad 'any short traditional poem sung, with or without accompaniment or dance, in assemblies of the people'. He has pointed out (*l.c.* 71) that, though the ballad traditions of most European countries were not to reach their apogee till the fifteenth and sixteenth centuries, balladry must have originated at a much earlier period:

> William of Malmesbury (he writes) states definitely that a poem about Canute's daughter Gunhild, falsely accused before her husband the Emperor Henry III, and unexpectedly delivered, was *nostris adhuc in triviis cantitata* (c. 1140). Brompton (c. 1350) names her accuser and defender, Roddyngar and Mimicon; Matthew of Westminster gives us Mimecan. There is no doubt that these references are to a poem of traditional nature and of content identical with the ballad of *Sir Aldingar*.

Various scraps of evidence such as this have led Entwistle to conclude that the origin of English and Danish balladry may with probability be dated to the mid-twelfth century, while the Greek balladry of Asia Minor may, in his opinion, have originated as early as the tenth century (*l.c.* 62–71).

The occurrence of Fionn ballads in the Book of Leinster (transcribed about the year 1160), in language a little older than that of the scribe, bears out the evidence cited by Entwistle indicating a date earlier than 1140 as the period of origin for west-European balladry in general.[1] It is indeed possible to regard Irish ballads as native developments of the speech-poems commonly inserted in Irish prose sagas and of the stories explaining placenames which appear naturally in certain learned *dinnsheanchus* poems. In view, however, of the close coincidence of dates in the rise of Irish balladry and of west-European balladry in general, it seems wiser to regard the Irish movement as connected essentially with the European.

The distinctive form of Irish ballads is, on the other hand, clearly due to the influence of the native speech-poem inserted in a prose saga. Both ballad and speech-poem are in Irish commonly known as *laíd* (Modern Irish *laoidh*); and Irish ballads, unlike those of the rest of Europe, are hardly ever told in the third person. They are, as it were, overgrown dramatic lyrics, in which the narrator of the story either takes part in its action or is closely connected with those who did so. They are normally regarded as having been addressed to St. Patrick by either Oisín or Caoilte, who are pictured as having long survived the other members of the Fiana. A clear forerunner of the Fionn type of ballad is indeed to be found as a speech-poem in the eleventh-century tale belonging to the Heroic cycle entitled *Síabur-charpat Con Culainn* (Cú Chulainn's Ghostly Chariot).

---

[1] Cf. especially *Óenach in-diu* (Book of Leinster, 206 b) and *Dám thrír* (207 b). *Óenach in-diu* appears also in slightly modernized form as poem XIII of the early-seventeenth-century *Duanaire Finn* (cf. also notes to poems I and XLVIII in *Duanaire Finn*, Part III). In *Duanaire Finn*, Part III, p. cxvi, a date c. 1100 has been assigned, mainly for linguistic reasons, to *Óenach in-diu* and four other Fionn poems. This date is not to be insisted on; a date between 1100 and 1140 is consonant with the evidence. On the other hand, the English precursor of the ballad of Sir Aldingar known to William of Malmesbury in 1140 was probably in existence well before 1140.

There Cú Chulainn, having returned from the dead in his ghostly chariot, recites to St. Patrick a long poem about his adventures in Lochlainn (Norway). This eleventh-century Cú Chulainn ballad addressed to St. Patrick may have served as a model for Fionn ballads in general, and more particularly for those of them which share its theme, an overseas expedition. It could well be that some twelfth-century Irishman, pleased by ballads he had heard sung either in England or the Norse settlements in Ireland, realized that the native *laíd* supplied a mould which might be used to the same purpose. Such union of a theme borrowed from without and developed in a manner that was wholly native would be quite in harmony with the Celtic mode of procedure in literature and art at all periods.

Not many of these twelfth-century Finn-*laídi* which remind one of ballads have been preserved. All of them might be classified as speech-poems in so far as the narrator refers to himself in the first person and is looked on as a companion of the principal actors. Some of them, such as Gráinne's poem for the sleeping Diarmaid, from which some quatrains have been cited in translation on p. 153, are purely lyrical and may in fact be speech-poems recorded apart from their prose context by a scribe. Another few would have caused no surprise even to a tenth or eleventh-century audience, their themes being mainly of learned interest, and, for the carrying on of learned as opposed to narrative tradition, verse had always been a recognized vehicle. Another small group, though new in so far as they are definite examples of verse narration of a story, are traditional in so far as they make Fionn's opponents magic beings; while a few others are more or less untraditional even in this respect, their main theme consisting of warrior feuds and battles. Yet others are a strange, typically Irish, amalgam of several of the different forms and spirits which have been referred to.

The two Book of Leinster poems mentioned in footnote

1 on page 158 are good examples of the group whose theme is the traditional Fionn theme of opposition to magic beings. The first begins *Óenach in-diu luid in rí* (To-day the king went to a fair) and tells how Fionn, exercising a black horse which had been given to him after he had admired its racing, at nightfall reached a house near Ballyvourney in Co. Cork:

> Fionn, ruler of the Fiana, said: 'There is a house which I have never seen before; Caoilte, I have never heard of a house in this glen, though I know the district well.'

Having sought entertainment in the strange house, they were tormented there throughout the night by a grey-haired giant, a three-headed hag, a headless man with one eye in his breast, and nine bodies with nine heads separated from them. At dawn the house disappeared and Fionn and his two companions, Caoilte and Oisín, arose unharmed. Fionn then discovered the identity of his tormentors; and from a prose account of the incident, which is either contemporary with the verse or a little earlier, we learn that it was by putting his thumb under his tooth of mystic knowledge and chanting a charm of the type known as *teinm laodha* (literally 'chewing of pith')[1] that Fionn made his discovery.

This is a forerunner of the *bruidhean* type of tale which will be discussed later in this section (pp. 185–7). The one-eyed phantom seems to be Fionn's chief opponent (*supra*, pp. 147, 149, 156) in an altered form, while the magic dwelling which disappears at sunrise is a commonplace of Irish folklore, literature, and hagiography.[2]

The second of the two Book of Leinster ballads under consideration begins with the line *Dám thrír táncatar i-lle* (They came here as a band of three). It has been edited by Stern in the *Festschrift Whitley Stokes Gewidmet* (1900),

---

[1] See O'Rahilly, *Early Ir. Hist. and Mythol.*, 338–9. For Fionn's gift of divining, see *supra*, p. 149, and *infra*, p. 186.

[2] *Duanaire Finn*, III, 29, 442.

8–12,[1] and tells of the strange visit to the Fiana of a triad of magic brothers with a marvellous hound who had the gift of converting water into mead or wine. The hound is identified in the ballad with the hound which Tuirinn Bicreo's three sons procured for use by Lugh before the Battle of Moytirra. This hound procured for Lugh already appears in an eleventh-century poem edited by Thurneysen in ZCP, XII, 244–245.[2] The strange parallel between the two magic triads has been commented on by Stern and Thurneysen (*ll.c.*) and forms an aspect of the wider Fionn-Lugh parallel which has been discussed *supra*, p. 147.

Prose variants of the stories told in the two Book of Leinster ballads we have been considering will be found in *Acallam na Senórach* which has been already referred to in this section (p. 157) as 'perhaps the most pleasing of the many pleasing products of Middle-Irish inventive genius'.

The first mention of *Acallam na Senórach* in Irish literature occurs in a recension of *Dinnshenchus Érenn* (The Place-lore of Ireland) belonging to the last quarter of the twelfth century. In that recension a poem on *Tonn Chlidna* is said to have been uttered by 'Caílte[3] in the time of Patrick in the course of the Colloquy (*Acallam*) they carried on concerning the placelore (*dinnshenchus*) of Ireland'. This proves that the *Acallam* was in existence in the last quarter of the twelfth century and that it was then regarded by the learned as essentially a branch of *dinnshenchus* literature. Modern folklorists might classify it as a *Rahmenerzählung* consisting of more than two-hundred anecdotes related by Caílte or Oisín to St. Patrick and others and set in the framework of a journey over Ireland. To a French medievalist its typically Irish form of prose interspersed with speech-poems (often now hardly distinguishable from narrative

---

[1] Cf. also ZCP, III, 433–4, for a later copy in the Book of Lismore.
[2] The poem is a forerunner of the Early Modern *Oidheadh Chloinne Tuireann*, discussed above, p. 109.
[3] The older spelling of modern Caoilte.

ballads) would suggest comparison with the form of *Aucassin et Nicolette*, which its thirteenth-century author describes as a *cante-fable*; while the student of Middle-Irish literature might well compare the *Acallam* to a reservoir into which a brilliant late-twelfth-century innovator had diverted several streams of tradition which previously had normally flowed in separate channels; for in the *Acallam* folk motifs, mythological motifs, warrior motifs, *senchus* (history) and *dinnshenchus*, lyric poetry, ballad poetry, and learned poetry, are found harmoniously united in a single whole.

In the section on Saga and Myth reasons have been given for regarding Irish storytelling as essentially oral. Among those reasons the antiquity of the original tradition, going back beyond the days of writing, and the imperfection of the manuscript versions of the tales held an important place. Now, though the *Acallam* undoubtedly contains traditional matter, and though even those episodes in it which are probably due to deliberate invention are always cast in the mould of one or other of the various ancient traditions, viewed as a whole it can only be regarded as a new untraditional creation. Moreover the twelfth-century portions of it which we possess are well narrated in the manuscripts and presented uniformly in a pleasing literary style. The first scribe of the original *Acallam* may therefore well have been its author, and it may have been perpetuated (after the manner of French and English medieval tales) largely by literary tradition rather than by oral tradition (such as typified most early Irish tales). That is to say, though the *Acallam* must have become known to the general public by means of oral recitation (either of the whole of it on successive nights, or of parts of it as occasion suited), the reciter may perhaps normally have derived his knowledge of it either directly, or at no very distant remove, from a manuscript.

We have no copy of the original *Acallam* which, as we have seen, seems to have existed about the year 1175, probably in a complete form. Two portions of recensions of it, which their language suggests should be assigned to some date about the year 1200, and an almost complete thirteenth- or fourteenth-century compilation based on them, are known to us from many manuscripts. The main portion is that edited under the title *Acallam na Senórach*, in 1892 by O'Grady, and in 1900 by Stokes, using different manuscripts. The second portion, which at least since 1870 has been known as the *Acallam Bec*, or 'Little *Acallam*', fills a gap in the O'Grady-Stokes *Acallam*, but envisages the wanderings of Caílte and Oisín somewhat differently. It was partially edited by Hyde in 1924. The thirteenth- or fourteenth-century version alters and harmonizes these older fragments, adds some additional matter, and slightly inflates the style, making it definitely less pleasing to modern readers. It was edited under the title *Agallamh na Seanórach* in three small volumes between 1942 and 1945 by Nessa Ní Shéaghdha, who has given a full account of the various versions in her introduction to volume I.

In adapting folk-themes to the grander or more realistic atmosphere he wishes to create the author of the *Acallam* sometimes has to gloss over inconsistencies or leave improbabilities unexplained.[1] When Caílte and his band of survivors from the Fiana first approached Patrick and his clerics, we are told that 'fear fell on them before the tall men with their huge wolf-dogs that accompanied them, for they were not people of one epoch or of one time with the clergy'. They were certainly not of one epoch with the clergy, for, according to the pseudo-historical account which the author of the *Acallam* clearly accepts, the Fiana flourished about the middle of the third century and Patrick lived about the middle of the fifth. It is clear that the author of the *Acallam* is here elaborating one of the many folktales which make Oisín survive so as to meet Patrick and to live with him. But the folktale-tellers have an explanation which is acceptable

---

[1] Cf. *infra*, pp. 184–7, and *Duanaire Finn*, III, p. liv.

when judged by folklore standards: Oisín had survived in the otherworld, where no one grows old or dies, having been enticed there by a fairy lover. The author of the *Acallam*, however, abandons this magic theme, unsuited to the romanticized yet fundamentally human atmosphere of his opening pages, and in consequence leaves his heroes' great age unexplained.

In due course Caílte is requested by Patrick to find a well which might be used to baptize the peoples of North Dublin and Meath. Having led Patrick to the well of Tráig Dá Ban (Two Women's Strand),

> Caílte began to tell its fame and qualities and made this *laíd*:

> Well of Tráig Dá Ban,
> lovely is your pure-topped cress;
> since your verdure has become neglected
> no growth has been allowed to your brooklime.

> Your trout out by your banks,
> your wild swine in your wilderness,
> the deer of your crags fine for hunting,
> your dappled red-bellied fawns.

> Your mast on the tips of your trees,
> your fish in the mouths of your streams,
> lovely is the colour of your sprigs of arum lily,
> green brook in the wooded hollow!

''Tis well,' Patrick said: 'hath our dinner and our provant reached us yet?' 'It has so,' answered bishop Sechnall. 'Distribute it,' said Patrick, 'and one half give to yon nine tall warriors of the survivors of the Fiana.' Then his bishops, and his priests, and his psalmodists arose and blessed the meat; and of both meat and liquor they consumed their full sufficiency, yet so as to serve their soul's weal.

Patrick then said: 'Was he a good lord with whom ye were; Finn mac Cumaill that is to say?' Upon which Caílte uttered this little tribute of praise:

Were but the brown leaf,
which the wood sheds from it, gold,
were but the white billow silver,
Finn would have given it all away.

'Who or what was it that maintained you so in your life?'
Patrick enquired; and Caílte answered: 'Truth that was in our
hearts, and strength in our arms, and fulfilment in our tongues.'[1]

It is difficult to refrain from quoting more of this delightful miscellany of prose and poetry, the greater part of which
is fortunately available to readers of English in O'Grady's
spirited translation. Many of the episodes end with a passage
such as the following which concludes the charming tale
of the marriage and death of Cáel the Valiant and his fairy
wife Créde:

'Success and benediction, Caílte!' Patrick said: ''tis a good
story thou hast told; and where is scribe Brógán?' 'Here am I.'
'By thee be written down all that Caílte hath uttered.' And
written down it was.

The *Acallam* fixed Fionn's literary background. Hence-
forward, without losing his old character of warrior-hunter-
seer, he is consistently represented as Fionn son of Cumhall,
leader of Cormac mac Airt's troops about the middle of the
third century. He is head of the House of Baoisgne, who
nourish an old grudge against the House of Morna headed
by Goll, who also belong to the Fiana. Between Fionn's
reconciliation with Goll (at the end of those boyhood
wanderings which have been mentioned on p. 156) and the
final breach, which resulted in the weakening of the Fiana
and their destruction at the Battle of Gabhair, a space is
left for the relating of tales of adventure and ballads. The

---

[1] The translation of the poem on Tráig Dá Ban has been taken from
Professor K. Jackson's *Studies in Celtic Nature Poetry* (1935), 15. (The
poem has four further quatrains in the original, in which legendary episodes
connected with the well are mentioned.) The translation of the matter
following the poem is that published by S. H. O'Grady, in his *Silva Gadelica*,
translation (1892), 104.

names of Oisín and Caoilte, who, in accordance with *Acallam* tradition, are pictured as surviving after the rest of the Fiana, are often used to give authority to these tales and ballads, which will be described later.

NEW TRENDS IN IRISH STORYTELLING AS A RESULT OF THE ANGLO-NORMAN INVASION

The author of *Acallam na Senórach* had been educated and had had his taste in literature formed in pre-Norman Ireland. It is hardly an accident, therefore, that the *Acallam* marks the culminating point of Old and Middle-Irish storytelling; for the Anglo-Norman invasion of 1175 put an end to the highkingship of Ireland and the provincial kingships, which had provided the patronage and background suitable for the preservation of the kingly themes of a past age; and in place of these kingships we ultimately find a number of petty lordships, ruled by Gaelic or by Gaelicized Norman lords. Irish literature therefore ceases to be so uniquely strange and unparalleled during the Anglo-Norman period (1200–1600) as it had been in the Old and Middle-Irish period (700–1200); for Ireland of the petty lordships being closer in many ways to contemporary medieval Europe than to ancient Ireland, it is hardly to be wondered at if its stories tend to manifest the same love of marvellous and romantic themes which we find in the contemporary *romans* of France and 'lying sagas' of Iceland. The Fionn cycle, being a cycle in which the marvellous had always had a place, and in which innovation had become the rule rather than the exception, was easily accommodated to the new spirit. A love-tale or a tale of marvel from the Ulidian cycle, such as the story of Deirdre and Naoise (*Oidheadh Chloinne hUisneach*), or the story of Cú Chulainn's training in arms (*Foghlaim Con Culainn*), could also remain popular; and folk themes, mythological themes, and borrowed themes could easily be used to form what for convenience may be called tales of the Romantic cycle, designed to while away an idle hour for medieval men and women gathered in an Irish nobleman's hall.

Till the late fifteenth century the change in taste is noticeable only in a more or less negative way. The matter of storytelling remains preponderatingly native, but the tales chosen for telling tend to be restricted to those which have a love-interest or can be filled out with marvellous incidents reminiscent of the folktale. The kingly grandeur, the genuine picture of ancient barbarism, and the unity of structure which mark so many Old Irish tales disappear in this period, and are replaced by a less grand tone, an unrealistic background, and a diffuse structure characterized by the piling of incident on incident. The unrealistic beauty of the Early Modern *Oidheadh Chloinne hUisneach* (Death of the Children of Uisneach), the manuscripts of which probably go back to a fourteenth-century recording of the tale, is, for instance, in marked contrast with the warrior realism which delights us in so much of its eighth- or ninth-century fore-runner, *Longes Mac nUislenn* (Exile of the Sons of Uisliu).[1] *Foghlaim Con Culainn* (Cú Chulainn's Training)[2] and *Tromdhámh Ghuaire* (Guaire's Burdensome Company)[3] are two other tales from the Ulidian cycle of which we have thirteenth-century versions. Both are characterized by the number of marvellous incidents which are narrated in them. The eighth-century King tale entitled *Echtra Fergusa Maic Léti* (The Journey of Fearghus son of Léide)[4] is likewise filled out in its thirteenth-century version, *Imtheachta Tuaithe Luchra agus Aidheadh Fearghusa* (The Proceedings of the People of Luchra and the Death of Fearghus),[5] by description of the marvels of the country inhabited by the tiny leprechauns (*luprucáin*): it may well be that this thirteenth-century version gave the Anglo-Irish Jonathan Swift the model for his account of the inhabitants of Lilliput.

---

[1] See above, p. 130.   [2] See above, p. 128.   [3] See above, p. 129.
[4] Cf. *Ériu*, XV, 33–48.   [5] Cf. *Éigse*, VII, 77.

The spirit of the mythological cycle, in a less kingly form than that which it had in the Old and Middle Irish periods, was eminently suited to the new trend, and along with re-tellings of older tales, it was enriched in the thirteenth, fourteenth and fifteenth centuries by tales such as *Eachtra Thaidhg Mheic Céin* (The Journey of Tadhg Son of Cian) (a story of the *Immram* type),[1] *Eachtra Airt Mheic Cuinn* (The Journey of Art Son of Conn) (a story of the fairy-lover type),[2] *Oidheadh Chloinne Tuireann*,[3] *Oidheadh Chloinne Lir* (The Death of the Children of Lir), and *Altram Tighe Dá Mheadhar* (The Fosterage of the House of Two Vessels). *Altram Tighe Dá Mheadhar*, probably composed in the fourteenth century, is of special interest to Arthurian scholars because, as Van Hamel pointed out, it shows native Irish Christianization of a pagan Celtic magic-vessel story, which makes it easier to believe that the Grail legend is likewise due to Christianization by a related Celtic people of a similar pagan theme. *Oidheadh Chloinne Lir*, which Professor James Carney believes to have been composed perhaps as late as the year 1500,[4] was popular with eighteenth-century scribes, who, grouping it with the fourteenth-century *Oidheadh Chloinne Tuireann* and *Oidheadh Chloinne hUisneach*, refer to the whole group as *Trí Truaighe na Sgéalaigheachta* (The Three Sorrows of Storytelling).

Towards the end of the fourteenth century it would seem that even in a Norman household in Ireland the repertory of Irish storytellers was still an almost wholly native one. Gearóid Iarla, third earl of Desmond, who died in 1398, still, for instance, refers only to native stories in his extant poems. In accordance with the taste of his time, however, the stories in which he was interested would seem normally to have had love for their theme. In almost every poem of the unpublished series by him contained in the fifteenth-

---

[1] See above, p. 113.
[2] Cf. *Fagháil Chraoibhe Cormaic mheic Airt* mentioned above, p. 136.
[3] See above, p. 109 and p. 161, n. 2.   [4] *Éigse*, VI, 107.

century Book of Fermoy[1] he refers to the story of Diarmaid and Gráinne (cf. *supra*, p. 152–4). And in one of them (poem 29, beginning on p. 167 of the manuscript) he refers to stories about (1) Gráinne and the son of Cochrann, (2) Aodh son of the king of Connacht, (3) the daughter of a king of Leinster, (4) Naoise (cf. *supra*, p. 166), (5) Cana, son of the King of Scotland, and Créidhe, daughter of Guaire (cf. *supra*, p. 138), and (6) Geilghéis, daughter of Guaire—all, except perhaps the second, apparently love-stories.

Some generations after Gearóid Iarla's day the positive contribution of the Anglo-Normans to Irish story-telling begins, however, to become evident. There was a period in the second half of the fifteenth century and the first half of the sixteenth when the Anglo-Norman lords in Ireland managed their own affairs with little control or interference on the part of the English government. During this period their adoption of Gaelic ways, which had already proceeded far, and their intermarriage and alliance with the Gaelic aristocracy increased greatly. It is not surprising, therefore, to find that the Franco-English culture which was their inheritance begins about this time to exercise a marked influence on Irish literature and storytelling.

In the well-known list made probably about the first quarter of the sixteenth century of the *nomina librorum existencium in libraria Geraldi comitis Kildarie*, twenty-one Latin, eleven French, seven English, and twenty Irish books are mentioned.[2] This list indicates the interest taken in Irish literature by a great Norman lord in Leinster in the period under consideration. The corresponding growth of Gaelic interest in matter of continental origin may be illustrated by comparison of the references to stories and *exempla* worked into their bardic poems by two poets of the Connacht Ó hUiginn family who lived respectively in the first half of the fifteenth and the second half of the sixteenth

---

[1] *Cat. of Ir. MSS. in the RIA*, p. 3110 sq.
[2] See O'Grady, *Cat. of Ir. MSS. in the Brit. Mus.*, I, 154.

century. In the twenty-six poems by Tadhg Óg Ó hUiginn (†1448) printed by Father Lambert McKenna in his *Aithdioghluim Dána* there are many references to stories about native kings and heroes, but none to stories or *exempla* of continental origin. In the forty-four poems by Tadhg Dall Ó hUiginn (†1591) published by Professor Eleanor Knott, on the other hand, as well as references to native tales, references may be found to Hercules, to Daedalus, and to the destruction of Troy, to a story from Mandeville's travels, to a tale about an emperor in Italy, a tale about a French knight's son, a tale about King Arthur, an anecdote about Walter Map, and continental fables and *exempla*. The contrast is striking; and examination of the contents of Irish manuscripts of the late fifteenth and following centuries suggests that it is not fortuitous; for Irish translations of continental religious and medical texts and of English or Latin versions of French works of fiction are often found in such manuscripts.[1]

TRANSLATIONS AND ADAPTATIONS

The continental fictional matter[2] by which Irish story-telling was enriched in translation or adaptation, during the fifteenth and sixteenth centuries, includes: Mandeville's travels and Marco Polo's travels; the Arthurian 'Quest of the Holy Grail';[3] the stories of William of Palerne,[4] Guy of Warwick, and Bevis of Hampton; *Seachrán na Banimpire* (The Wandering of the Empress), being an Irish version of the story of *Florent et Octavian*; *Gabháltus Séarluis Mhóir*

---

[1] See R. Flower, *Ireland and Medieval Europe* (1927).

[2] For references to editions or manuscripts of most of these texts, and of the texts of native Romantic tales to be mentioned in the following pages, see Dr. Best's two bibliographies and the Index (by R. Flower and Dr. M. Dillon) contained in Volume III of the *Catalogue of Irish Manuscripts in the British Museum*.

[3] Ed. as *Lorgaireacht an tSoidhigh Naomhtha* by Miss S. Falconer, 1953.

[4] Ed. by Miss C. O'Rahilly, 1949.

(Charlemagne's Conquest) based on the Latin account of Charlemagne fictitiously attributed to Turpin; the story of *Fierabras*, likewise belonging to the Charlemagne cycle; and *Stair Ercuil* (The History of Hercules), based on Caxton's English translation from the French of Raoul Lefevre. *Eachtra Mhacaoimh an Iolair* (The Adventures of the Lad carried off by an Eagle), and *Eachtra Ridire na Leómhan* (The Adventures of the Knight of the Lions),[1] are sixteenth-century tales of the *roman d'aventure* type which seem to be based on unidentified French originals. The seventeenth-century *Eachtra Mhelóra agus Orlando* (The adventures of Melora and Orlando)[2] may have drawn the name Orlando and its central theme (a warrior maiden's rescue of her lover from imprisonment with the help of a magic object) from cantos III–IV of Sir John Harrington's English translation of Ariosto's *Orlando Furioso*; but the Irish author cast the whole in an Arthurian framework and filled the theme out with incidents drawn both from his imagination and from native literature and folklore. To these translations and adaptations of French and Italian tales, Father Manus O'Donnell, about the end of the seventeenth century, added translations of three tales from the Spanish of Juan Perez de Montalvan.[3]

Translations and adaptations such as those mentioned explain the tendency to make eastern countries such as Greece, Syria (*Sorcha*),[4] and Persia the theatre for adventure in native tales; for, ever since the Crusades, adventures in those lands were a commonplace of continental fiction. The Scandanavian countries as another favourite theatre for Irish adventure-stories have, however, an older foundation; for

[1] Ed. by A. Ní Chróinín, 1952.
[2] Ed. by M. Mhac an tSaoi in her *Dhá Sgéal Artúraíochta* (1946), and also (with fuller discussion of the sources) by Miss A. M. E. Draak in *Béaloideas*, XVI, (1946), 3–48.
[3] Preserved in RIA MSS, 23 M3 and 23 M 10.
[4] Sometimes (like the northern *Ioruadh*) a merely mythical land with no precise geographical situation.

Lochlainn (Norway) already fulfils that function in the eleventh-century *Síaburcharpat Con Culainn,* which has been referred to *supra,* p. 158.

IRISH ARTHURIAN TALES

Lorgaireacht an tSoidhigh Naomtha (*supra,* p. 170, n. 3) is the only direct translation of a well-established Arthurian tale preserved in Irish manuscripts. Nevertheless that Irish storytellers were familiar with other less religiously inspired specimens of the Arthurian cycle is proved by the use of Arthurian characters or themes in narrative literature composed in Ireland from the fifteenth century on. The fifteenth-century *Eachtra an Mhadra Mhaoil* (Adventures of the Crop-eared Dog) is, for instance, an Arthurian story composed in Ireland in which Sir Gawain (in Irish Sir Bhalbhuaidh) helps the Crop-eared Dog, who is really the son of the King of India, to recover his human shape, having defeated his enemy the Knight of the Lantern. The story woven around this theme is a loosely constructed collection of marvellous happenings and metamorphoses in Egypt, Greece, Scythia, *Sorcha,* and other countries.

Céilidhe Iosgaide Léithe (The Visit of the Grey-hammed Lady)[1] is another fifteenth-century Irish addition to the Arthurian cycle. It tells how the King of Gascony, having come to Arthur's court under the assumed name of *Ridire na Sealga* (The Hunting Knight), pursued a deer on three successive days. On the third day the deer revealed herself to him as a woman. She came on a long visit to the court, and the ladies there ultimately grew jealous of her. She confided the secret of what she said was her nickname, *Iosgad Liath* or 'Grey Ham', to a special friend among the ladies. The friend betrayed her confidence, and the stranger was accused publicly by the ladies of the court of having a horrid tuft of grey hair behind her knee. When all had raised their

[1] Ed. by M. Mhac an tSaoi in her *Dhá Sg. Artúraíochta* (1946), 42–70.

dresses above their knees, however, the stranger was the only one who had no such tuft. The women were punished, and the men of Arthur's court having had strange otherworld adventures in regions such as the Plain of the Scarlet Hazels (*Magh na gColl gCorcra*) were provided with new wives by their mysterious visitant. *Céilidhe Iosgaide Léithe*, references to which in Irish documents suggest that it was a highly-thought-of story, is told in the true native style with intermingling of pleasing speech-poems in the prose narrative.

Poem LXV in *Duanaire Finn* seems to represent late-fifteenth-century transference to the native Fionn cycle of the popular Arthurian story of the chastity-testing cloak, well known in England from the ballad of the *Boy and the Mantle*.

The Arthurian section in the fifteenth- or sixteenth-century *Eachtra Mhacaoimh an Iolair*, already mentioned on p. 171, may, as Flower has suggested,[1] have been added by the Irish author to the unidentified French tale on which that *Eachtra* is based; and the Arthurian framework of *Eachtra Mhelóra agus Orlando*, mentioned on the same page, is almost certainly of Irish origin.[2]

Eachtra an Amadáin Mhóir (The Adventures of the Great Fool) is an Early Modern Irish prose Arthurian tale, of uncertain date, connected in some obscure way with both the Perceval story and the story of Sir Gawain and the Green Knight. *Laoidh an Amadáin Mhóir* (The Lay of the Great Fool) is a poetic version of the same theme, not expressly associated with the Arthurian cycle. The relationship of the Lay to the prose *Eachtra*, and of both to a Scottish Gaelic folk-version of the Great Fool's adventures, has not yet been satisfactorily clarified.[3]

[1] *Catalogue*, II, 354.
[2] Cf. also the Arthur episode in *Caithréim Conghail Chláiringnigh*, mentioned *infra*, 175.
[3] Cf. *Studies*, XXXVII (1948), 368–371.

Though the Arthurian cycle was thus clearly not unfamiliar to the Irish storyloving public in the late Middle Ages, it never in Ireland assumed the important place in literature which it did in other medieval countries. The tendencies of the human mind which derived satisfaction from the otherworldliness of its magic forests, disappearing castles, and mysterious kings and maidens, were already amply satisfied in Irish storytelling by the Mythological tales and Fionn tales, in which many of the motifs of the Arthurian cycle are preserved in forms closer to the forms they had in the lost Celtic tales from which Arthurian tales, Fionn tales, and Mythological tales are all three descended.

IRISH ROMANTIC TALES

When scholars speak of the Romantic tales of Early Modern Irish they are thinking mainly of a group of tales whose main traits are the prevalence of magic and the piling of unbelievable incident on incident. They are akin in this respect to the wonder-tales of native folklore. Moreover the chief actors in them, though not quite so undefined as the chief actors in folktales, tend, as in the folktale, to be mere pegs to which the themes and motifs used may be attached. They resemble French thirteenth-century *romans d'aventure* in so far as knightly adventures in distant lands, and the winning of wives, are normal features in them. Tales of the type we are considering are common in seventeenth- and eighteenth-century manuscripts, but many of them were certainly in existence in the sixteenth century; and the sixteenth and seventeenth centuries may be looked upon as the period in which they enjoyed their greatest popularity. Unlike the translation literature and the Arthurian tales, their appeal was to a very wide public, as the recording of versions of many of them from Irish and Scottish-Gaelic storytellers in the course of the last century proves. Their closest parallels in European literature are the Icelandic 'lying sagas' of the thirteenth and following centuries.[1] Whether the resemblance is due to independent grafting, in both Icelandic and Irish storytelling circles, of the French thirteenth-century *roman d'aventure* to vigorous native traditions, or whether the Hebridean gallowglasses (*gallóglaigh*, literally 'Norse warriors'), who were employed as their heavy-armed troops by Irish lords from the thirteenth century on, were familiar with the Icelandic type of tale and introduced it to Ireland, is uncertain.[2]

The chief hero in a tale of this type may connect it with the King cycle, or with those later developments of the cycle which have been mentioned in section II above, p. 139, n. 1. Examples of such connection are to be found in: *Caithréim Conghail Chláiringnigh* (The Triumphs of Flat-nailed Conghal), which tells of the winning of the kingship of Ireland by a legendary Ulidian king after warrior episodes in Ireland and Rathlin, a magical folkloristic episode in Norway, and an Arthur episode in England; the unpublished *Eachtra Chonaill Ghulban*, which describes the romantic adventures in eastern lands of Conall Gulban, fifth-century founder of the Tír Chonaill dynasty;[3] *Tóraigheacht Duibhe Lacha* (The Rescue of Dubh Lacha), which tells of Dubh Lacha's love for the magically-gifted Mongán mac Fiachna, the east-Ulster king who died in 625; *Eachtra Chléirigh na gCroiceann* (The Adventures of the Skin-clad Cleric), which tells of the coming in hideous guise of the god Aonghus an Bhrogha to test the chastity of the wife of Conghal Cinn Mhaghair, king of Ireland, who died in 710; *Eachtra an Cheithearnaigh Chaoilriabhaigh* (The Adventures of the Narrow-striped Kern), which tells of the coming of the

[1] Cf. E. Mogk, *Geschichte der norwegish-isländischen Literatur* (1904), 831, 845 sq.; Åke Lagerholm, *Drei Lygisögur* (1927); B. S. Phillpots, *Edda and Saga*, 239 sq.

[2] Professor J. H. Delargy tentatively suggests the second possibility in his *Gaelic Story-teller* (1945), 38–39.

[3] For another tale with the same title see *infra*, p. 191, n.1.

god Manannán in the guise of an ill-clad kern, or light-armed soldier, to play tricks on various early-sixteenth-century Irish lords; *Díthreabhach Glinne an Pheice* (The Hermit of Gleann Péice), *Leigheas Coise Céin* (The Healing of Cian's Leg), and *Giolla an Fhiugha* (The Lad of the Ferule), all telling of fairy adventures which befell Murchadh son of Brian Bóraimhe (†1014), or his companions; *Bás Cearbhaill agus Farbhlaidhe* (The Death of Cearbhall and Farbhlaidh), being the story of the mutual love of Farbhlaidh, daughter of a fictitious James king of Scotland, and of an Irish poet Carrol O'Daly.[1]

Certain other Irish Romantic tales have some fictitious non-Irish character for their main hero.

To this class belongs *Eachtra Iollainn Airmdheirg* (The Adventures of Red-weaponed Iollann), other names for which are *Tóraigheacht Fhiacoil Ríogh Gréag* (The Rescue of the Tooth of the King of Greece) and *Sgéal Úcaire na Seachtmhaine* (The Story of the One-week Fuller). *Eachtra Iollainn Airmdheirg* tells how the youngest son of the King of Greece, having descended to the underworld in a basket let down by ropes, recovered the tooth which had been knocked out of his father's mouth. Abandoned in the Underworld by his treacherous brothers he succeeded in escaping. Returning to Greece he disguised himself for a week as a fuller and thus won back the bride he had nearly lost and showed up the treachery of his brothers.

Eachtra Chloinne Ríogh na hIoruaidhe (The Adventures of the Children of the King of Ioruadh) tells how Cod and his two brothers, sons of the King of the mythical Ioruadh, have strange adventures in places such as Italy, Greece, *Sorcha*, and the Forest of Wonders, as they search for an enchanted lady who has laid them under *geasa* or 'magical bonds' to discover her in her native home. Cod in the end becomes King of the World; his brother Cead becomes King

[1] This tale is referred to in a late-sixteenth-century poem, *Éigse*, VII (1953), p. 89 (q. 10), p. 93 (notes to 10 and 11).

of Ioruadh; and Míchead, the third brother, becomes King of Greater Asia.

Tóraigheacht an Chairthe Sgárlóide (The Pursuit of the Rock of Scarlet Cloth), also known as the Story of Dark Síoghra, is a tale of the *iomramh* type.[1] It tells how a mysterious visitor to the court of the King of Norway was offended by the treatment given him. The visitor's name was Síoghra Dubh (Dark Síoghra). To take vengeance on the King he enticed him on a voyage to visit an overseas region in his dominions, of the existence of which the King had been unaware. The first episode on the voyage reminds the reader of the story of Iollann Airmdhearg. In it the two sons of the King descend successively in a box to the Underworld, almost as Iollann descended in a basket. The younger of the two, Earca Astalla, behaves well in the underworld and is rewarded by obtaining for his father the object of his quest, namely the *cairthe sgárlóide*, or 'rock of scarlet cloth', which had the power of dyeing in one of three colours any clothing which touched it; Earca incidentally won for himself a Tuatha Dé Danann wife. In the following episodes visits to magic islands are described, in which thousands of the King of Norway's warriors are successively slain. When the fleet finally reaches the place of which Síoghra had spoken, the King of Norway himself and what was left of his troops, with the exception of Earca Astalla, are slain. Síoghra, having rescued Earca Astalla, returns with him to Norway.

In the late seventeenth century, some Ulster author, or school of writers, wrote romantic tales about the heroes of the Ulidian cycle. To this group of tales belong: *Tóruigheacht Ghruaidhe Grian-sholus* (The Rescue of the Lady of the Sun-bright Cheek), edited by Miss Cecile O'Rahilly; *Eachtra na gCuradh* (The Adventures of the Heroes) and *Coimheasgar na gCuradh* (The Combat of the Heroes), edited by M. Ní Chléirigh; and the first four tales in the

[1] Cf. *supra*, p. 168, n. 1.

volume entitled *Sgéalta Rómánsuíochta* (Romantic Tales), edited in 1952 by M. Ní Mhuirgheasa and S. Ó Ceithearnaigh—the fifth tale in that volume is a story of similar type attached to the Fionn cycle. Battles in foreign countries and magical themes borrowed from Irish folklore form the basis of this group of tales.

The further development of the Romantic cycle at the hands of eighteenth-century authors such as Tadhg Ó Neachtain and Mícheál Coimín lies outside the scope of this work.

As may be concluded even from this summary description of them, Early Modern Irish Romantic tales are often, either in whole or in part, a raising of the simple folklore suited for peasants, with its anonymous hero and unsophisticated background, to a form which could please an audience accustomed to stories about a hero defined by name, place, and period, and with a background in which the higher ranks of society would not object to find themselves. *Eachtra Iollainn Airmdheirg*, for instance, is little more than a variant, with a *roman d'aventure* background, of the international folktale listed as 301 in A. Aarne and S. Thompson's *Types of the Folk-tale* (1928);[1] and one episode in *Tóraigheacht an Chairthe Sgárlóide* is, as we have seen, more or less modelled either on *Eachtra Iollainn Airmdheirg* itself or its folk predecessor. Again, in an episode of the Romantic *Caithréim Conghail Chláiringnigh*, Bé Iúda, daughter of the King of Norway, demands as her bride-price 'the three birds of the daughter of Cairtheann Corr—and the men and

---

[1] The international folktale has been described as 'the tale of the youth who liberates three princesses from a subterranean prison, but is himself left underground by his faithless brothers or companions and soon afterwards escapes and unmasks the traitors' (cf. R. Flower, *Cat. of Ir. MSS in the British Museum*, II, 360). Both the pure folktale, and the folk versions of the Iollann variant of it, have been recorded from Irish oral tradition: see *Béaloideas*, VIII (1938), 97–99, XII (1942), 125; *Leabhar Sheáin Í Chonaill* (S. Ó Duilearga) (1949), 417, 466–467. A Tartar *shamans'* variation of the theme is referred to in *Studies* (1940), 538–539.

women of the earth would sleep, though they were in dire distress, by reason of the music of those birds—and the yoke of Cearb's chariot, and the helmet of Misceanmhas.'[1] Now, to set a difficult task as the condition of winning a bride is a folktale commonplace. In a Mayo tale, for instance, recorded by E. Mhac an Fhailghigh in *Béaloideas*, IX (1939), 98 sq., a king asks a poor woman's son to obtain for him as the price of his daughter 'the Sword of Light possessed by the giant yonder in his castle and three grey hairs which are in his head'. The themes of the Conghal episode and the folk episode are, then, similar; but the contexts are typically different. The characters in the Conghal episode are made definite by name, time, and place; Bricne (otherwise 'Bricriu') appears in it in his traditional role of mischiefmaker; the chief characters are all of distinguished birth and act and speak after the manner of warrior princes. The hero of the folktale, on the other hand, is a poor woman's son and in his boyhood was a cripple; many of the characters are anonymous, while the hero's name, Maghnus, is a name and nothing more.

That the particular group of tales we have been considering on pp. 174–9 are of comparatively late origin is certain; and that such tales were not highly thought of till continental influence had begun to exercise its main effect on Irish storytelling in the late fifteenth century is equally certain. That similar tales, formed by the application of folk themes to characters drawn from the Hero and King cycles, had been popular in certain circles from very early times is, however, probable. The overseas expedition and magical adventures of the Middle Irish *Tochmharc Eimhire*, on which the thirteenth-century *Foghlaim Con Culainn* was based,[2] would almost lead one for instance, if it had been composed in the fifteenth century, to classify it with the Romantic tales. The tenth-century Ulidian tale entitled *Fled Bricrenn*

---

[1] *Caithréim Conghail Cláiringnigh*, ed. P. M. MacSweeney (1904), 110.
[2] See above, p. 128.

ocus Longes Mac nDoíl Dermait (The Feast of Bricriu and the Exile of the Sons of the Beetle of Forgetfulness) is an older and even clearer example of a tale more akin in spirit and construction to Early Modern Romantic tales than to Old and Middle Irish Heroic tales, with which, by reason of its main character, Cú Chulainn, it is normally found convenient to classify it. It has even less claim, however, to be classified with the Heroic tales than *Caithréim Conghail Chláiringnigh* has to be classified either with them or with the King tales.

Like the *Caithréim* and Early Modern Romantic tales in general, *Fled Bricrenn ocus Longes Mac nDoíl Dermait* has a well-defined aristocratic background which serves to distinguish it from the true folktale. Cú Chulainn is its chief character, and it opens with an account of a feast prepared by Bricriu reminiscent of the feast of the more famous *Fled Bricrenn* discussed in section II above, pp. 118–22. Bricriu claims that, before eating his feast, the Ulidian warriors should perform exploits (here we seem to have a native Irish form of the feast-motif with which Arthurian adventures are often introduced). The twelve Ulidian warriors present set out to wreak slaughter; but the story as recorded is confined from this point on to the adventures of one only among them, namely Cú Chulainn.

After several adventures (summarized briefly in the manuscript but doubtless narrated at length in real tellings of the tale),[1] Eocho Ronn, king of Uí Maine, the winning of whose daughter by Cú Chulainn has just been described, says, 'May you have no ease of sitting or lying, Cú Chulainn, till you discover what took the three sons of Dóel Dermait from their country.'

Here we have the common folk motif of the imposition of a hard task to win a bride, which we have already considered in the Norway episode of *Caithréim Conghail Chláiringnigh*. The very form of its imposition reminds one of the formulae used by modern folktale-tellers when in

---

[1] Cf. above, pp. 98–101.

similar circumstances the hero is forbidden 'to eat two meals
at one table or to sleep two nights on one bed' till injunctions
laid on him have been fulfilled. The task itself is like that
of seeking 'knowledge of the unique tale about women'
(*fios fátha an aoin-sgéil ar na mnáibh*),[1] which is commonly
joined in certain Irish folktales to the task of winning the
giant's Sword of Light (*claidheamh solais*). It is also similar
to the task of discovering 'what robbed the Knight without
Hair or Laughter of his hair and his laughter', imposed on
the hero in the Irish folktale of the *Ridire gan Ghruaig gan
Gháire*;[2] and in at least one Donegal version of the Ridire
tale, in which the *Ridire* (knight) is called a *Gruagach* (a
well-known type of magic person), the task of discovering
why his laughter has ceased is actually the condition of
winning a king's daughter.[3]

Cú Chulainn has many strange adventures, including
visits to magic islands, before he discovers the story of the
sons of Dóel Dermait. Unfortunately the story itself, which
should clearly be told before line 250 of Windisch's edition,[4]
is left untold in the only version preserved, nor does the
conversation with the sons of Dóel Dermait, referred to in
line 291, occur where one might expect to find it, in the
middle of line 265, before reference to the return of Dóel
Dermait's sons to their own country as the result of Cú
Chulainn's defeat of their magic enemy. Had the story and
the conversation been recorded by the tenth-century redactor of the manuscript version, we should doubtless have
found it as strange and gruesome as the story of the fate
that befell the Ridire's sons, whose restoration to the Ridire
in the modern folktale, following the hero's defeat of their
magic enemy, restored to him also his lost laughter.

The opening feast, the piling of incident on incident, the

[1] Cf. *Duanaire Finn*, III, p. xvi (line 24), pp. 196–197.
[2] *Leabhar Sheáin Í Chonaill* (S. Ó Duilearga), 428; *Duanaire Finn*, III,
pp. xviii, 50, 183.
[3] *Béaloideas*, II (1930), 408.
[4] See his *Irische Texte*, II, i (1884), p. 175.

hard task imposed to win a wife, the overseas journey, the magic islands, and the general folkloristic setting of *Fled Bricrenn ocus Longes Mac nDoíl Dermait*, suggest, then, strongly that tales akin to Irish Romantic tales, and to the British tales on which the Arthurian romances are founded, were popular in certain circles in Ireland long before the Early Modern Romantic tales attained the position of pre-eminence accorded them by Irish men of letters in the sixteenth and seventeenth centuries.

LATER FIONN TALES

In discussing the changes brought about in the spirit of Irish storytelling as the result of the Anglo-Norman invasion,[1] it was pointed out that the Fionn cycle was easily accommodated to the new spirit, being a cycle in which the marvellous had always had a place, and in which innovation had become the rule rather than the exception. It is not easy to assign dates to the Fionn tales of this period. The classical language of Early Modern Irish professional poetry had a more or less fixed form from the beginning of the thirteenth century to the middle of the seventeenth. This classical language set a standard towards which even writers of prose tended to conform, though some scribes and authors occasionally used more modern forms, and some authors liked to give an air of antiquity to their compositions by occasional use of Late Middle Irish forms. Early Modern Fionn tales are on the whole preserved to-day only in manu-scripts belonging to the seventeenth and following cen-turies, though it is certain that most of the tales are older than the seventeenth century. It is this universal tendency towards standardization, and the occasional tendency towards archaism, joined to the generally late date of the manuscripts, which renders it difficult to arrange Early

---

[1] *Supra*, p. 166.

Modern Fionn tales with any degree of certainty in a dated series.

The thirteenth- or fourteenth-century story of the Slaying of the Pig of Formaoil and the Death of Fionn[1] is told more or less after the manner of learned Late Middle Irish King tales. The continuously popular story of Diarmaid and Gráinne has already been referred to *supra*, pp. 152–4, 169. Accounts of fighting in distant lands and of the winning or recovering of wives suggest that certain other Early Modern Fionn tales have been influenced directly or indirectly by the *roman d'aventure* and are therefore hardly earlier than the late fifteenth century. To this class belong *Tóraigheacht Taise Taoibhghile* (The Pursuit of the Gentle White-sided Lady), *Tóraigheacht Shaidhbhe Inghine Eóghain Óig* (The Rescue of Sadhbh Daughter of Young Eóghan), and *Eachtra Iollainn Iolchrothaigh Mheic Ríogh na hEasbáinne* (The Adventures of Many-beautied Iollann son of the King of Spain), also known as *Bás an Mhacaoimh Mhóir* (The Great Youth's Death). The amusing *Eachtra Bhodaigh an Chóta Lachtna* (The Adventures of the Churl with the Grey Coat) is certainly as late as the sixteenth century and is probably modelled on *Eachtra an Cheithearnaigh Chaoilriabhaigh*, whose theme, the visit of a deity in disguise,[2] it shares with several Irish stories which include *Eachtra an Ghiolla Dheacair* (The Adventures of the Difficult Lad), a famous Fionn tale composed probably in the fifteenth century. *Cath Fionntrágha* (The Battle of Ventry) is known to us in a form contained in a fifteenth-century manuscript and also in a later form contained in eighteenth and nineteenth-century manuscripts; the author of the late-twelfth-century *Acallam na Senórach* (*supra*, p. 161) was also familiar with a version of this story.[3]

---

[1] See *Duanaire Finn*, III, 136, where it is pointed out that the title 'The Chase of Síd na mBan Finn and the Death of Finn' given this tale by K. Meyer, *Fianaigecht*, pp. xxxi and 52, is misleading.

[2] Cf. *supra*, p. 175 , and Flower, *Cat.*, II, 340–1.   [3] Flower, *l.c.*, 394.

Authors of Early Modern Fionn tales such as those mentioned in the preceding paragraph draw freely on folklore. In this they remind one of the authors of the Romantic tales; but while borrowing from folklore is in keeping with the folk origin of the Fionn cycle[1] and was always a feature of it, in the Romantic cycle it is probably to be explained largely as being based on the model set by Fionn tales and lost tales of the type to which *Fled Bricrenn ocus Longes Mac nDoíl Dermait* belonged.[2]

In *Cath Fíonntrágha*, for instance, the fighting against foreign invaders, in spite of daily slaughter, continues for a whole year, but the refilling of the depleted ranks of the invading army, which seems to be postulated, is left without explanation. If we take it that the literary tale is based on an ancestor of the West Kerry folktale of the Everlasting Fight at Ventry[3] we have a convenient explanation of the problem. In the folktale, in accordance with a well-known Irish folk-motif, the warriors of the enemy army are resuscitated during the night by a magic hag. The omission of this important feature from the literary tale would be in keeping with the tendency often manifested by learned storytellers to avoid the more obviously naive traits of the folk matter on which they draw.[4]

Again, the in-tale of how Iolann won his wife, told in *Eachtra Iollainn Iolchrothaigh Mheic Ríogh na hEasbáinne*, reminds one of similar uses of the in-tale to prolong and diversify the main plot in Romantic tales such as *Díthreabhach Glinne an Phéice*, *Leigheas Coise Céin*, and *Eachtra Chonaill Ghulban*. The model on which such use of the in-tale is based may have been found in the in-tales which form an essential feature of the international folkstory known in Ireland as *Sgéal an Ghadaighe Dhuibh* (The Story

---

[1] Cf. *supra*, p. 145.　　　[2] Cf. *supra*, pp. 179–82.
[3] Cf. *Duanaire Finn*, III, p. xxxiv, n. 1.
[4] Cf. *supra*, p. 163, n. 1, and p. 179, *infra*, pp. 186–7 and *Duanaire Finn*, III, p. liv.

of the Black Thief), numbered 953 in the Aarne-Thompson list.[1]

The weird horse which in *Eachtra an Ghiolla Dheacair* carried fourteen of the Fiana to the Otherworld likewise has what are in many ways older analogies in the horses of Fionn folktales which carry people to dwellings of the dead.[2] Such horses occur also in the folklore of countries other than Ireland, and the motif, like many other folk motifs, is doubtless an ancient one preserved independently in various countries of Indo-European culture.[3]

Though folklore and mythology are not convertible terms, folk themes and mythological themes are freely inter-changeable. The *bruidhean* theme, which is a feature of Early Modern Fionn lore, seems to be a theme which in origin was mythological but has been preserved in Ireland mainly by folk tradition. It relates how Fionn was enticed to a magic dwelling (*bruidhean*) and how he suffered ill-treatment there. Folklore preserves it in a form in which its original mythological connections are evident and which makes it almost certain that the original *bruidhean* was an otherworld dwelling equivalent to the Greek Hades.[4]

A twelfth-century forerunner of the *bruidhean* type of tale has been discussed earlier in this work, p. 160. *Bruidhean Chaorthainn* (The Rowan-tree Dwelling), *Bruidhean Chéise Corainn* (The Dwelling at Céis Chorainn) and *Bruidhean Eochaidh Bhig Dheirg* (Little Red Eochaidh's Dwelling) are clear examples of the type. *Eachtra Lomnachtáin* (The Adventures of the Naked One), *Cuireadh Mhaoil Uí Mhanannáin* (The Invitation issued by the Bald One descended from Mannanán), as well as the framework in

---

[1] Cf. T. F. O'Rahilly's references to these tales, *Gadelica*, I, 276 (n.1), 280–3.

[2] Cf. *Duanaire Finn*, III, pp. xxxii–xxxiii. (The reluctance to accept Dr. Krappe's identification of the Otherworld with the realm of the dead, expressed by me on those pages, is hardly justified.)

[3] Cf. *Duanaire Finn*, III, p. xliv, lines 28–31 and notes 3–5.

[4] See *Duanaire Finn*, III, pp. xxiii–xxxiii.

which are set the many tales of *Feis Tighe Conáin* (The Feast in Conán's House), and two of those tales themselves, are less clear examples. *Bruidhean Bheag na hAlmhan* (The Little Fight at Allen), on the other hand, is a tale of a quarrel between rival groups of the Fiana and has nothing to do with the theme under consideration except that the word *bruidhean*, in its secondary meaning 'quarrel', is used in the title.[1]

From the *bruidhean* group, the Irish historian Geoffrey Keating, writing in the early seventeenth century, chose out *Bruidhean Chaorthainn* as being typical of unhistorical Fionn tales.[2] *Bruidhean Chaorthainn* was first written down probably in the sixteenth century, and is apparently based on a folk-tale of the Lorcán Mac Luirc type discussed in *Duanaire Finn*, III, p. xxiv sq.; but in it we find that raising of folk-tale marvel to the heroic and pseudo-historical levels which characterizes all such use by learned storytellers of matter derived from folklore. In paragraphs 20–21 of *Bruidhean Chaorthainn*, for instance, when Fionn had learnt by chewing his thumb[3] that the King of the World and armies from Greece and other countries had come to help the King of Norway's son to destroy him and his companions in the *bruidhean* in which they had been stuck to the earth by magic,

> the little band of nobles of the Fiana who were in the *bruidhean* uttered sorrowful sad cries by reason of the troubles and trials that surrounded them.
>
> 'Cease, Fiana of Ireland,' said Fionn, 'and become not as mourning women because the hour of your death has arrived; but take heart and courage and sound our Fian chant for us sadly and sweetly as music before death.'
>
> Then they closed their lips together and sounded the Fian chant for Fionn and for themselves.

[1] For a fuller list of folk and literary tales which conform to the *bruidhean* pattern, *see Duanaire Finn*, III, p. 26, n. 1.

[2] Keating, *Foras Feasa ar Éirinn*, ed. Dinneen, II (1908), 326.

[3] Cf. *supra*, pp. 149, 160.

Such passages in the heroic spirit are far removed in tone from the naive marvels of the folktale which the author of *Bruidhean Chaorthainn* used as his model.[1]

Recognizing the special excellence of this learned Fionn lore, folktale-tellers often added tales of this class to the Fionn tales already current among the common people, as the repertories of modern unlettered storytellers in Ireland and Gaelic Scotland prove. By the sixteenth century, therefore, when the Ulidian tales, with few exceptions, had long been outmoded, and Romantic tales, though well known, were too indefinitely characterized to form a unified concept in men's minds, *Fianaigheacht*, popular with all classes of Gaelic society and connected with one clearly defined group of traditional figures, had come to represent what was typically native in storytelling; and when Máiri nighean Alasdair Ruaidh in the seventeenth century mentions *greis air uirsgeil na Féinne*[2] as the regular ending to the feast, the board-games, and harping, which followed a day spent in hunting by a lord of the Scottish MacLeods, her words, applied to the household of a sixteenth- or seventeenth-century Irish lord, would doubtless remain equally true.

LATER FIONN BALLADS

Early Modern Ossianic balladry[3] contributed even more than the prose tales to give the Fionn cycle the pre-eminent position which it has held among Gaelic speakers in Ireland and Scotland from the fifteenth century to the present day. Till the late seventeenth century the Gaelic literature of these two countries had not been differentiated, and the two finest collections of Early Modern Fionn ballads we possess are contained in an early-sixteenth-century Scottish manuscript and an early-seventeenth-century Irish manuscript.

[1] Cf. *Folkliv*, 1938, pp. 213–5, and *supra*, p. 184, n. 4.

[2] 'A period devoted to telling tales of the Fian,' *Gaelic Songs of Mary MacLeod*, ed. by J. Carmichael Watson (1934), line 283.

[3] For the origin of Ossianic balladry see *supra*, pp. 157–62, 165.

The Scottish manuscript was written in very peculiar spelling by Sir James MacGregor, Dean of Lismore in Argyll, and by his brother Duncan, mainly from oral tradition, in the first quarter of the sixteenth century. This *Book of the Dean of Lismore* is the best anthology of Early Modern Gaelic poetry (Irish and Scottish) that has ever been gathered into a single volume. About twenty of the poems contained in it belong to the Fionn cycle. The Irish manuscript was written in Louvain and Ostend, in the year 1627, by Aodh O'Doherty for his patron Captain Sorley MacDonnell of Antrim, an officer in the Spanish army of the Netherlands. It is entitled *Duanaire Finn* (The Poem-book of Fionn) and all its sixty-nine poems belong to the Fionn cycle. Countless Irish and Scottish manuscripts of the eighteenth and nineteenth centuries contain versions of several of the items found in these early collections, along with many other Fionn ballads. Some of these extra ballads are doubtless as old as many of those contained in the *Book of the Dean of Lismore* and in *Duanaire Finn*. A few, however, were hardly composed before the seventeenth century, and some imitations, such as Mícheál Coimín's famous *Laoidh Oisín ar Thír na nÓg* (Oisín's Lay concerning the Land of the Young), are as late as the eighteenth century.

The themes of the Early Modern ballads resemble those of the Romantic tales and prose Fionn tales which have already been described. They might be classified under headings such as *síodh*-ballads, *bruidhean*-ballads, ballads of magic visitors, invader-ballads, ballads of internecine strife, pursuings and rescues, elopements, foreign expeditions, monster-slayings and hunts. But it is less their theme than their poetic excellence which gives them value, and a lover of poetry who has even a rudimentary acquaintance with the Irish language and Irish metre is certain to be delighted by them. Some of them are almost wholly narrative; some pass freely from a lyric to a narrative mood; while others, such as the sixteenth- or early-seventeenth-century Lay of the Blackbird of Derrycarn, are almost pure lyrics with a slight narrative flavour. Perhaps a translation of that Lay, with citation of the Irish of the first quatrain in which its half-rhymes or assonances are marked by special print, will give a better idea of the charm of Ossianic balladry than could be achieved by mere description or analysis:

> *Binn sin, a luin Doire an* Chairn!
> *Ní chuala mé i n-*aird *san* BHITH
> *ceól ba binne ná do* ghuth
> *agus tú fá* bhun *do* NID.

Sweet your song, blackbird of Derrycarn! Nowhere in the world have I heard music sweeter than your voice, as you sing beneath your nest.

Sweetest music in all the world,—it would be sad not to listen to it for a while, son[1] of Calpurnius of the sweet bells; and you could turn again to your nones.

If the true story of the bird were known to you as it is to me, you would shed tears bitterly, and would cease for a while to think of God.

In the blue-streamed land of Norway, the son of Cumhall of the red goblets got the bird which you now see. There you have its true story.

That wood to the west of Derrycarn, where the Fian used to rest. Because of the beauty and loveliness of its trees the blackbird was put there.

The singing of the blackbird of Derrycarn, the belling of the stag from the Berried Cliff, made music to which Fionn would sleep in the early morning, along with duck from the Lake of the Three Narrows.

Grouse around Conn's Cruachain, the whistle of the otter of the Ridge of Two Lakes, the cries of the eagle of the Phantom's Glen, the calling of the cuckoos of the Hill of the Flowers.

The bayings of the hound of Glenkeen, and the scream of the blind hunting eagle, the noise of the morning wave coming in from the Strand of the Red Stones.

When Fionn and the Fian lived, moorland was dearer to

---

[1] i.e. St. Patrick; cf. *supra*, pp. 158, 163.

them than church. Sweet to them was the song of blackbirds; the sound of bells they thought not sweet.

Old ballads are often lengthened in the later manuscripts by insertion of extra verses of dialogue. Occasionally these extra verses preserve something of the spirit of the late-twelfth-century *Acallam na Senórach*. In a late addition to the sixteenth-century *Laoidh Chnuic an Áir* (Lay of the Hill of Slaughter), for instance, Oisín, urged by Patrick to tell the truth, replies:

> We of the Fiana never told a lie. Falsehood was never attributed to them. But by truth and the strength of our hands we came safe out of every combat.[1]

The mutual understanding and goodwill which characterize the relations between Oisín and Patrick in *Acallam na Senórach* had, however, gradually been replaced during the thirteenth and following centuries by misunderstanding and opposition.[2] In some of the late additions which we are considering, the misunderstanding is increased, and in particular Oisín, shows himself naively unaware of the true implications of Christianity:

> Were my son Osgar and God (he says) engaged hand to hand on this hill to the west, if I were to see my son Osgar down, I should admit that God was a strong man.[3]

That quatrain has considerable poetic merit; but at times the opposition of saint and pagan descends to mere buffoon-ery, adapted to the taste of the humbler folk into whose keeping the old tradition had passed after the overthrow of aristocratic Ireland in the seventeenth century.

Ossianic ballads were originally sung to simple airs with a wandering rhythm, reminiscent of plain chant and suited

---

[1] For the original Irish see P. Ó Siochfhradha, *Laoithe na Féinne* (1941), p. 29, q. 59. With the thought compare the last sentence of the passage from the *Acallam* cited *supra*, p. 165.
[2] See *Duanaire Finn*, III, 56.   [3] Ó Siochfhradha, *l.c.*, p. 85, q. 51.

to the rhythms of their syllabic metre. These comparatively free rhythms of syllabic metres differ greatly from the fixed rhythms of present-day Irish song-metres, which can be sung to the regularly-barred music of modern times. The tradition of singing Ossianic airs died out in Ireland in the nineteenth century, but still survives among a few of the older generation of singers in western Scotland.

MANUSCRIPT TRADITION AND ORAL TRADITION

In the section on Saga and Myth above it was pointed out that most Old and Middle Irish storytelling had an oral origin and was probably carried on orally with little or no reference to the manuscript versions of the tales recorded by men of monastic learning. On p. 162 of the present section, on the other hand, it has been suggested that the first scribe of *Acallam na Senórach* may have been its author, and that reciters of the *Acallam* may have derived their knowledge of it either directly, or at no very distant remove, from a manuscript. Some of the translations and adaptations of continental fictional matter which have been discussed in this section were probably purely literary and never entered into oral tradition. The same may be true of a few learned compositions such as the semi-historical *Eachtra Chonaill Ghulban*, written in archaic language in the late-sixteenth- or early-seventeenth century and edited by Father Lehmacher, ZCP, XIV (1923), 212–69.[1] In the early-nineteenth century, O'Grady informs us,

> tales used to be read aloud in farmers' houses on occasions when numbers were collected at some employment, such as wool-carding in the evening, but especially at wakes. Thus the people became familiar with all these tales. The writer has heard a man who never possessed a manuscript, nor heard of

[1] This tale is quite distinct from the Romantic *Eachtra Chonaill Ghulban* mentioned *supra*, pp. 175, 184, which is included in the repertories of many unlettered storytellers to-day.

O'Flanagan's publication, relate at the fireside the death of the sons of Uisneach without omitting one adventure, and in great part retaining the very words of the written versions.[1]

The reading aloud of tales described by O'Grady can hardly have been general before the seventeenth century when the use of paper permitted the multiplication of manuscripts. But it is certain that, from the fifteenth century on, lay men of learning, in close touch with storytellers of the aristocratic tradition, both wrote and used manuscripts. It is not surprising, therefore, to find that Early Modern tales recorded by such scribes seem to be closer in form to what was really told than are the manuscript forms of tales of the Old and Middle Irish period, when manuscripts were mainly monastic and scribes were interested in the historic rather than the aesthetic value of the matter they recorded. It is significant in this respect that in describing Early Modern tales in this section it was nowhere necessary to surmise how certain passages used to be really told or how lacunae were to be filled, whereas when the analogy of some of them with the Middle Irish *Fled Bricrenn ocus Longes Mac nDoíl Dermait* was being pointed out[2] it was on several occasions necessary to indulge in such surmising.

It is possible, therefore, that, from the fifteenth century on, manuscripts played a definite part in the carrying on of Irish story-tradition; and many tales, even among those which became popular in oral tradition, may have been written before they were told, as has been suggested may have been the case already with the late-twelfth-century *Acallam na Senórach*. On the other hand, in discussing an important episode in *Leigheas Coise Céin*, O'Rahilly has drawn attention to the fact that 'In this, as in some other respects, the Scottish oral versions of *Leigheas Coise Chéin* preserve what must have been the original form of the tale

[1] S. H. O'Grady, *Tóruigheacht Dhiarmuda agus Ghráinne* (Transactions of the Ossianic Soc., III, 1857), 29.

[2] *Supra*, pp. 180–1.

more accurately than does the fifteenth-century manuscript version.'[1] This would go to show that some at least of the Early Modern tales belong as wholly to an essentially oral tradition as the Old and Middle Irish tales discussed in *Saga and Myth in Ancient Ireland*. Whether oral or literary in their origin, however, we may be certain that all Irish tales and ballads, with the few exceptions already mentioned in this section, were intended primarily to be told or chanted rather than to be read.

[1] *Gadelica*, I, 282, n. 1.

Books for further reading

Rudolf Thurneysen, *Die irische Helden- und Königsage* (1921).

Myles Dillon, *The Cycles of the Kings* (1946); *Early Irish Literature* (1948).

Thomas F. O'Rahilly, *Early Irish History and Mythology* (1946).

H. M. and N. K. Chadwick, *The Growth of Literature*, I (1932).

Robin Flower, *Ireland and Medieval Europe* (The Sir John Rhŷs Memorial Lecture, British Academy, 1927).

James H. Delargy, *The Gaelic Story-teller* (The Sir John Rhŷs Memorial Lecture, British Academy, 1945).

Kuno Meyer, *Fianaigecht* (1910).

Duanaire Finn, Part III (Introduction, etc., by Gerard Murphy) (1953).

Valuable discussions by Robin Flower of sources, parallels, etc., will be found in the *Catalogue of Irish Manuscripts in the British Museum*, Vol. II (1926), to which the Index, by Robin Flower and Dr. Myles Dillon, in Vol. III (1953), may be used as a guide.

James Carney, *Studies in Irish History and Literature* (1955).

A full bibliography of all but very recent publications will be found in Dr. Best's two volumes: National Library of Ireland, *Bibliography of Irish Philology and of Printed Irish Literature* (compiled by R. I. Best) (1913); and R. I. Best, *Bibliography of Irish Philology and Manuscript Literature, publications 1913–1941* (1942).

INDEX OF NAMES, TERMS,
AUTHORITIES, ETC.[1]

[1] As the words indexed deal with different periods in Irish literature, there is necessarily a certain mixture of early and modern orthography in the indices, e.g. *Aonghas, Óengus*. It has frequently been necessary to index an item, found in different spellings in the texts, under an arbitrarily chosen compromise form.

INDEX OF TALES, ETC.